To Niki

with very best wishes

Peter Carrington

Lent 3
08 March 1990
St. Paul's Knightsbridge

GOOD AND FAITHFUL SERVANTS

by

Peter Galloway and Christopher Rawll

GOOD AND FAITHFUL SERVANTS

All Saints' Margaret Street and its Incumbents

by

Peter Galloway
and
Christopher Rawll

**CHURCHMAN PUBLISHING LIMITED
WORTHING**

1988

"Well done, good and faithful servant; you have been faithful over a little, I will set you over much; enter into the joy of your master"
Matthew 25:21

Good and Faithful Servants
by Peter Galloway and Christopher Rawll

was first published in Great Britain in 1988

by CHURCHMAN PUBLISHING LIMITED
117 Broomfield Avenue, Worthing
West Sussex BN14 7SF

Publisher: E. Peter Smith

and Distributed to the book trade
by BAILEY BOOK DISTRIBUTION LIMITED
Warner House, Wear Bay Road
Folkestone, Kent CT19 6PH

ISBN 1 85093 104 6

Typeset by CPJ Fotoset Limited and printed by
VR Litho both of
Worthing in the County of West Sussex

Dedications

to the memory of
Frederick Oakeley
1802–1880
who laid the foundations
on which others have built
P.J.G.

to Douglas Richardson
who laid the foundations
of my faith
C.C.G.R.

Acknowledgements

Our thanks go to the following individuals who contributed to the appearance of this book.

The late Dr Eric Arnold, Director of Music at All Saints', 1968–1988, whose memory stretched back to the last years of Henry Mackay; Michael Brough, a godson of Kenneth Ross; The Reverend Father David Campbell, SSJE; Miss Diana Compton-Bracebridge, a great grand daughter of Berdmore Compton; The Reverend Canon Gordon Hopkins; The Reverend Richard Buck, Assistant Curate 1968–1974; The Reverend Peter Delaney; Denzil Freeth, Churchwarden of All Saints'; The Reverend Prebendary John Gaskell, Assistant Curate 1964–1968; Mrs Veronica Goldberg-Steuart, a great grand daughter of Berdmore Compton; The Right Reverend David Hope, Bishop of Wakefield; The Reverend David Hutt; Sister Jean Margaret and Sister Margaret, both of the Society of All Saints; The Right Reverend Michael Marshall; the late Dr Hermia Mills, for her memories of Dom Bernard Clements; Dom Augustine Morris, OSB; Mrs Margaret Osmaston, a grand daughter of William Whitworth; The Right Reverend Edward Roberts, Assistant Curate 1931–1935; The late Reverend Tom Ryder, Assistant Curate 1936–1941; The Reverend John Slater, Assistant Curate 1970–1977; Miss Sheila Sparrow, sister of David Sparrow; The Reverend Desmond Tillyer; Mr Malcolm Underwood, archivist of St. John's College, Cambridge; The Reverend David Vickery, Assistant Curate 1958–1963; The Reverend Father Harry Williams, CR, Assistant Curate 1945–1948.

Our thanks also go to Miss Mary Mathias, who typed the manuscript.

London   Peter Galloway
July 1988   Christopher Rawll

i

FOREWORD

By the Most Reverend and Right Honourable Robert Runcie,
Archbishop of Canterbury

All Saints, Margaret Street has long possessed a renown which has transcended the reputation of its successive incumbents. This is as it should be. The story of a parish church is not merely the story of its clergy. Yet, from the beginning, the Vicars of All Saints have been remarkable men, and that this book of biographies should be produced at all is a tribute to their collective quality.

I have known the six most recent incumbents of All Saints. Each has cherished the three characteristics I always associate with this famous church. The best known, and perhaps most widely appreciated, is the meticulous care taken over the offering and presentation of worship. There is reverence to be found in this church, and I believe that it is only in reverence for God that reverence for the rest of His creation is held secure.

A second characteristic, equally appreciated but perhaps not so widely known, is the place given to spiritual direction. An ordered Christian life complements ordered Christian worship. The incumbents of All Saints have never shirked their duty in commending the centrality of discipline in Christian discipleship.

Thirdly, All Saints has valued preaching and its clergy have not neglected this means of nourishing the Christian mind. Whilst worshippers might glimpse something of the mystery of God in the glory of the liturgy, no latter day mystery religion has been on offer here. The intellect, and the challenges it often throws up for Christian faith, has not been ignored, and from this pulpit has been proclaimed a faith in which both reason and revelation have been given an honoured place.

If future incumbents of All Saints continue to cherish these characteristics they will not only be honouring the tradition of this church but ensuring the validity and relevance of its witness in each new age. I am grateful to Peter Galloway and Christopher Rawll for this enterprising and illuminating account of the Vicars of All Saints and I hope that this volume's readership is as extensive as the reputation of these clergy is deserved.

iii

FOREWORD

By the Right Reverend and Right Honourable
Graham Leonard, Bishop of London

I HAVE always felt that my association with All Saints' began not in 1962, when I became Archdeacon of Hampstead (the Archdeaconry then included St. Marylebone), but by a kind of extended presbyteral apostolic succession in 1952. In that year, I became Vicar of Ardleigh in Essex of which Canon T. W. Perry had been a distinguished incumbent from 1872–1891. He had been Curate of All Saints' from 1850–1855 and was a recognised authority on the Ornaments Rubric in the Book of Common Prayer, serving on the Royal Commission on Ritual from 1867–1870.

When I arrived in Ardleigh, I found a number of relics of his incumbency, including the printed card with the service on one side and eucharistic hymns on the other, which he had prepared for congregational use when he introduced a Sung Eucharist at 8 a.m. on Sundays. The card was strictly Prayer Book on the one hand and richly Catholic on the other.

I begin in this way because the card affords early evidence of the tradition of All Saints' and of its influence throughout the country. People often speak of All Saints' as the quintessentially "high church". The "highest in churchmanship that one is likely to find in the Church of England" is how one writer describes it. No one would describe All Saints' as 'low' or 'central' but to give it the palm of being the highest is to ignore its particular and distinctive character which is so amply demonstrated in this admirable and fascinating account of the Vicars of the parish.

Particularly during the second half of the nineteenth century, 'high' churches tended to fall into two types. On the one hand were parishes where the Prayer Book rite was followed using what was rudely described by its critics as British Museum ceremonial and which was intended to follow the pre-Reformation English practice of the Sarum rite, in attempts to be distinctively Anglican. On the other hand were parishes where the eucharistic rite derived much from the Roman Catholic rite expressed with ceremonial also derived from the then ancient Roman Catholic use.

At All Saints', the Prayer Book rite for both the Mass and the Offices has always been followed but it has been clothed in Western ceremonial meticulously and beautifully expressed. Behind this practice has been a firmly held conviction that it is possible to worship and live as Catholic in the Church of England which is an integral, though distinctive, part of the one Holy Catholic and Apostolic Church. That being so it is proper and natural to express that worship in a living tradition which is shared by the majority of Catholic Christians in the West.

As is clear from the book, successive incumbents have in their various ways, witnessed by their teaching, preaching and sacramental and pastoral care, to the claims of the Church of England to be a church in which – to use the words of Vatican II – "the Catholic Church subsists" and within which a full Catholic and Christian life is possible.

It is significant and characteristic that Fr. Ross's book *Why I am not a Roman Catholic* begins with the famous quotation of Geoffrey Fisher when Archbishop of Canterbury: "We have no doctrine of our own – we only possess the Catholic doctrine of the Catholic Church, enshrined in the Catholic Creeds; and those creeds we hold without addition or dimunition". To that truth, which needs to be proclaimed and heard today, All Saints' has stood valiantly in large measure because of those Vicars, whose work is so splendidly recorded in this book by Peter Galloway and Christopher Rawll, to whom we are greatly indebted.

PREFACE

ON 5 July 1839 Frederick Oakeley, Fellow of Balliol College, Oxford, was licensed by the Bishop of London as Minister of Margaret Chapel, a small proprietary chapel in Margaret Street in the West End of London. In the early months of 1839 Oakeley, under the influence of John Henry Newman and others, had openly committed himself to the principles of what was to become known as the Oxford Movement. Finding himself at odds with the Master of Balliol and life at the College increasingly difficult, he was tempted by the offer of the chapel in London and consulted Isaac Williams, Newman's Curate at the University Church of St. Mary the Virgin. Williams urged him to accept the offer. "I thought that the Chapel was a sphere best suited for him and where he might do us much good . . . And he took the Chapel on my advice. Little did I foresee the issue and change that was to come; but I represented to him that his abilities suited him well for stating our views and principles in London".*

Oakeley stayed at Margaret Chapel for only six years, leaving in the summer of 1845 shortly before being received into the Roman Catholic Church. But during those few years he laid the foundations of what has become one of the most prominent churches in London – All Saints', Margaret Street. Almost one hundred and fifty years after the beginning of Oakeley's ministry the work that he started still continues, on the same site though in a different building, and a word of thanks should go to Isaac Williams who, by prompting Oakeley into accepting the offer of Margaret Chapel can be credited, at least partially, with inaugurating the work of the Oxford Movement in London.

In producing this book about the first twelve Vicars

---

*The Autobiography of Isaac Williams, edited by Sir George Prevost, London 1893, pp. 86–87.

of All Saints' who have faithfully continued and developed Oakeley's work in Margaret Street, our intention was to produce brief sketches of the lives of the twelve men responsible for 'stating the views and principles' of the Oxford Movement at the place in London where it began. We have not attempted thorough and detailed biographies of each man, preferring rather to concentrate on his years at All Saints', and occasionally touching on other relevant aspects of his life. We hope that a collection of portraits has emerged telling something of the personality, interests and work unique to each while at the same time drawing parallels and common strands and themes. We had no desire either to be adulatory about their talents and strengths, or to be ruthless in exposing their faults and weaknesses. The dearth of information about certain of the subjects in certain periods of their lives has led us to some speculation but, as far as possible, we have tried to be objective and factual in our survey. If we seem to be prejudiced in our examination of a life or an incident, then we can only say that it was unintentional.

The contributions of the Archbishop of Canterbury and the Bishop of London to our book are themselves tributes to Frederick Oakeley and his twelve successors, and to the work of the Oxford Movement in Margaret Street during the past century and a half.

Contents

Frederick Oakeley, Minister of Margaret Chapel, 1839–1845

THE TRACTARIAN
FREDERICK OAKELEY
1839–1845

"I can honestly say that the motive which actuated me in trying to improve upon the ceremonial practice . . . was to give worship as much reverential beauty as was consistent with the strict observance of such rubrics as were plain and incontrovertible, and the free interpretation of others which seemed to me to admit without undue straining of a more catholic sense than that which they commonly received . . . I must maintain that the ritual at Margaret Chapel, whatever may be said for or against it, was simplicity itself . . . no Catholic, however uneducated, could possibly have mistaken the Communion Service at Margaret Chapel for High Mass."

(Frederick Oakeley writing in 1879 shortly before his
death)

FREDERICK OAKELEY

Born: 5 September 1802
Christ Church, Oxford 1820–1827
Fellow of Balliol College, Oxford 1827–1845
Minister of Margaret Chapel 1839–1845
Roman Catholic 29 October 1845
St Edmund's College, Ware 1846–1848
St George's Cathedral, Southwark 1848–1850
Rector of St John's, Islington 1850–1880
Died: 30 January 1980

ON Monday 30 June 1845, Sir Herbert Jenner Fust, Judge of the Court of Arches, the Provincial Court of Canterbury, delivered his final judgement on a case which had occupied the mind of the Court for nearly one month. It was given in the Hall of the Advocates at Doctors' Commons in Knightrider Street, a small street connecting Godliman Street and Peter's Hill, on the south side of St Paul's Churchyard. Doctors' Commons (officially the College of Advocates and Doctors' of Law) contained both the Ecclesiastical and Admiralty courts, together with the advocates who practised there. These advocates were a wholly separate body from barristers, and were required to hold doctorates in civil law from Oxford or Cambridge before being admitted to practise in the Court of Arches. As Dean of the Arches, Sir Herbert Jenner Fust was ex-officio President of the College.

The case, Hodgson v. the Rev. F. Oakeley, had been instigated by Charles James Blomfield, Bishop of London, in an effort to deal finally with a priest in his diocese who for six years had been a source of some considerable embarrassment to him. Frederick Oakeley (1802–1880), the son of a baronet who had served with distinction in the East India Company in the last quarter of the eighteenth century, had gone up to Christ Church, Oxford, in 1820, and after some effort, had succeeded in securing election as a Fellow of Balliol College in 1827. During the next twelve years of his residence in Oxford, he came in contact with some of the brightest and most adventurous minds of his time, at a point when a wind of change was beginning to sweep through the University and the Church of England. Like so many of his contemporaries he gradually succumbed to the irresistable fascination of John Henry Newman, Vicar of the University Church of St Mary the Virgin 1828–1843, a towering intellectual genius of the 19th century.

Oakeley's election to Balliol coincided with the coming together of minds like Newman, Edward Pusey, John Keble, Hurrell Froude and others into an amorphous gathering known ever since as the Oxford Movement. The movement drew its inspiration from the sermon of John Keble delivered at the University Church on Sunday 14 July 1833 before His Majesty's Judges of the Assize. Keble was moved to protest against the interference of the State in the affairs of the Church, as manifested by the decision of the government to suppress certain of the archbishoprics and bishoprics of the Church of Ireland, a move which Keble denounced as national apostasy.

From that sermon grew a movement which was to change the image and spirituality of the Church of England, recalling it, through liturgy, music and devotion, to its Catholic heritage from days before the 16th century Reformation, and awakening in it a new zeal and sense of purpose not seen since the growth of Methodism in the 18th century. The Oxford Movement succeeded in firing the Church of England with a vision of the past glorious history of the Church and a commitment to bring that past to bear on the present and the future, transforming the Church of England beyond recognition by the end of the 19th century.

Today, the Movement is remembered mostly for the changes it wrought in the outward appearance of Christian worship. The revival of the use of vestments, incense, lighted candles, only intended to add dignity to the beauty of Christian worship, now taken for granted, led to widespread disagreement and quarrelling at the time. For the bold priests who, with the support of their congregations, were determined to introduce such things, hostility and riotous behaviour could be expected from certain quarters. Few of the bishops at the time had sympathy with the Movement and its aims, regarding it as little

4

more than a manifestation of the kind of superficial 'popery' which had been expelled from the Church of England, root and branch, at the Reformation. Many priests found themselves constantly in dispute with their bishops over what now would be seen as the most minor matters. Such was the position of Frederick Oakeley.

Oakeley was a shy, kind and gentle person who might have passed his days peacefully as the scholarly Oxford don that most of his friends expected him to be. Slightly built, and lame, he was a much loved figure both in Oxford and London throughout his life. Oakeley committed himself to the principles of the Oxford Movement in the early months of 1839, and in the summer of that year he left the University to take charge of a small and architecturally unattractive proprietary chapel in the West End of London, his mind filled with the ideas he had learned from Newman, Pusey, Froude and others.

Licensed on 5 July 1839, he took up residence at 74 Margaret Street, London, across the road from his new charge, a mid-eighteenth century building known sometimes as Margaret Street Chapel, but more often as Margaret Chapel. The building had been constructed in about 1760 for a group of Deists under a certain Dr Disney. It had a chequered career under a succession of independent preachers as a centre of Deism. It was closed in the 1780s and then purchased and re-opened as a proprietary chapel of the Church of England in 1789. It continued with a succession of resident priests as an independent chapel within the parish of St Marylebone, but virtually nothing is known of its history until the 1820s.

Margaret Street is in what is now called the West End of London, though in Oakeley's day it would have been called West London. It lies to the north of, and runs parallel with Oxford Street, connecting

Wells Street with Cavendish Square. It was laid out in 1734 and named after Lady Margaret Cavendish, wife of the 2nd Duke of Portland. It was not a particularly attractive or elegant street. Oakeley described it as being "devoid of romantic interest and ecclesiastical prestige as any other member of that peculiarly dull family of highways which occupies the neighbourhood of Cavendish Square".[1]

Margaret Chapel itself was not of a high architectural order, and the one surviving drawing of its exterior gives it the appearance of an eighteenth century meeting house for Dissenters. Oakeley described it as "a complete paragon of ugliness . . . it was low, dark and stuffy; it bore no other resemblance to the Christian fold than that of being choked with sheep pens under the name of pews . . . it was begirt by a hideous gallery, filled on Sundays with uneasy schoolchildren".[2] The pews stretched almost across the width of the Chapel, there being no central aisle, leaving two narrow passage ways, scarcely wide enough for two people to walk abreast, leading to what should have been the sanctuary, but which was occupied by an enormous three-decker pulpit reaching almost to the ceiling, with a small communion table hidden behind it.

Here, in this unpromising arena for experiment, Oakeley introduced a style of liturgy and music changing the Chapel beyond all recognition, transforming it into a model church of the Oxford Movement, and establishing the tradition of the church as it remains to this day. The three-decker pulpit was the first to go. The altar was adorned with a crimson frontal and a cross and candlesticks. A choir was formed, and before many months they were singing Gregorian Chant. A triptych was placed above the altar and eventually the pews were removed. Morning and Evening Prayer were said daily and, at least in his own private chapel in 74

6

Margaret Chapel

Margaret Street, Oakeley appears to have said the
full Roman Office. The congregation bore all these
changes with surprising equanimity, and with few
exceptions they became devoted to their Minister and
his distinctive liturgical ways. He was not without
friends and supporters, including William Gladstone,
and soon gathered around himself a considerable
number of people with varying degrees of influence
who attempted to shield him from the irritation of
Bishop Blomfield who viewed the happenings at
Margaret Chapel with some alarm. Blomfield's
patience was finally stretched too far when, in 1845,
the quixotic Oakeley addressed a letter to him,
claiming the right to hold, though not to teach, all
Roman doctrine. This was too much for Blomfield
who initiated the proceedings in the Court of Arches.

Believing that the Court would find judgement against him, whatever defence was put up, Oakeley refused to contest the case and resigned his licence on 3 June.

The inevitable judgement was delivered on Monday 30 June 1845. Without any counsel to defend him, the hearings turned into a dialogue between the judge and the prosecution. Fust felt that he must, "for the sake of the public, inflict such a punishment as may have the effect of preventing others from falling into the same errors into which Mr Oakeley has suffered himself to be led".[3] Fust ruled that Oakeley's licence "be revoked, and that he . . . be suspended from all discharge and function of his clerical office and the execution thereof".[4] "I direct that notice of this sentence be published in the usual manner at the Chapel in Margaret Street, on Sunday next the sixth day of July".[5]

CHAPTER ONE

THE FOUNDER
WILLIAM UPTON RICHARDS
1845–1873

'Almost alone in this great city he proclaimed Christ's Catholic faith in its integrity, and developed those living sacramental ministries of Christ's Church.'

('The Parting of Elijah and Elisha', a sermon preached at All Saints', Margaret Street on Sunday 22 June 1873, after the death of William Upton Richards.)

William Upton Richards, Minister of Margaret Chapel, 1845–1849, All Saints' 1849–1868, 1st Vicar 1868–1873

WILLIAM UPTON RICHARDS

Born: 2 March 1811
Exeter College, Oxford 1829–1833
Manuscript Department, The British Museum
1833–1849
Deacon 1836   Priest 1837
Curate of Bushey 1836–1837
Assistant Minister, Margaret Chapel 1837–1845
Minister of Margaret Chapel 1845–1849
Incumbent of All Saints', Margaret Street 1849–1868
Vicar of All Saints', Margaret Street 1868–1873
Died: 16 June 1873

SUCH was the situation faced by William Upton Richards when he was appointed to succeed Oakeley as Minister of Margaret Chapel in 1845.

Richards was born on 2 March 1811, the only son of William Richards, of Penryn, Cornwall, and his wife, Elizabeth Rose Thomas. Of his childhood in Cornwall we know virtually nothing. Apparently his health was never strong enough for him to attend a public school and he was sent to Archdeacon Burney at Greenwich for private tuition for several years. He matriculated from Exeter College, Oxford in 1829, graduating in 1833, his cousin, Dr Richards, being head of the college at that time. One of his contemporaries wrote of him at the time, "His character was as good as his most earnest admirers in after life could have wished it to be. He was the same then that he was through life. He had the same goodness and cheerfulness which attached so large a circle of friends to him".[1]

After graduating, he was appointed an assistant in the Manuscript Department of the British Museum where he compiled an index to the Egerton MSS and the Additional MSS acquired by the Museum between 1783 and 1835. He was ordained deacon in 1836 and priest in 1837 by Bishop Blomfield of London. At the time of his ordination, Blomfield, one of the trustees of the British Museum, appointed him a sub-Librarian. He also spent a short time as curate to Dr Richards, now at Bushey in Hertfordshire, before moving to be Assistant Minister, at Margaret Chapel in 1837 where he remained for the last thirty-seven years of his life.

The task faced by Richards when he was appointed to succeed Oakeley in 1845 was daunting and difficult, and there were many who predicted that Oakeley's achievements would rapidly and irretrievably disintegrate. The powerful influences of Roman proselytism, now spearheaded by Oakeley, lay on one side, and on the other, the undisguised suspicion with which Margaret Chapel and its work were regarded by Bishop Blomfield. Oakeley had made Margaret Chapel the showcase of the liturgical practices of the Oxford Movement and succeeded in focusing public attention on the place. Having made the decision to become a Roman Catholic on 29 October 1845, Oakeley was clear in his own mind that this was the best course for all his supporters to follow and, initially, he tried to make a determined effort to persuade his former congregation to follow him. At Advent 1845, Richards wrote to Edward Pusey at Oxford telling him that "Oakeley has been doing in more than one case just what you say, and has been telling people that Margaret Chapel will soon be shut up and so forth, trying thereby to induce them to follow him, however much satisfied they may be with their present position – Is not this sad and trying to me? . . . With respect to Margaret Chapel I am determined by God's blessing to continue it . . . At all events there will be daily prayers come what will".[2]

The congregation were greatly distressed at the departure of Oakeley, but a number of them were determined that the Chapel should not be closed and that it should be maintained as a place of divine worship according to the traditions which had become so dear to them. They approached Bishop Blomfield who agreed to licence Richards as Minister of the Chapel. This was an act of surprising generosity on the part of the Bishop, an act matched by his wish that the Chapel services should continue as they had done under Oakeley. It is doubtful if the Bishop would have agreed to this move if the congregation had not presented him with their plans to continue the Chapel. The Chapel was held on leasehold from the Crown Estate, and the lease was due to expire on Lady Day 1848, when the site would revert to the Crown. As far back as 1842 Oakeley had proposed to negotiate the purchase of the freehold from the Crown and a sum of £2000 had been collected by the time of his departure, but nothing had been done. Now matters were more pressing. The exterior of the Chapel was in a dilapidated state, and the Bishop would have been justified in simply closing the Chapel until the expiry of the lease, when the site would then have reverted to secular purposes. But such was the zeal, devotion and tenacity of the congregation in those two years, that the site was saved, and on it were to be laid the foundations of one of the great centres of Christian prayer and worship in central London.

Upton Richards himself decided that one way to inject a sense of purpose and future into the congregation would be to remodel the interior of the Chapel, despite the fact that the exterior was in such bad shape. A remodelling would further improve the celebration of the liturgy while at the same time going some way towards erasing the memory of Frederick Oakeley by altering the appearance of the chancel in which he had ministered so successfully for six years. Such is the paucity of description and illustration of the Chapel in Oakeley's time that we find it impossible to give a detailed description of the changes. It is unlikely that there were any major structural alterations to the building, the majority of the work being directed towards a refurbishment and redecoration of the interior. We do not know for how long the Chapel was closed, except that it was reopened on All Saints' Day 1846. The sermon at the re-opening service was preached by the Reverend Henry Wilberforce, brother of Bishop Samuel Wilberforce of Oxford who had been a regular visitor to the Chapel in Dodsworth's day. It may have been at this time that the decision was taken to dedicate the proposed new church to All Saints. Oakeley's intention had been to dedicate the church to the

Virgin Mary. Had he remained within the Church of England, the building would be known today not as All Saints', but as St Mary's, Margaret Street.

By the beginning of 1849 and after a number of generous donations, the sites of the chapel and three adjoining houses were acquired for the sum of £9,000. William Butterfield was appointed architect and the Ecclesiastical District of All Saints' was formed by Order-in-Council dated 30 July 1849. The Act of Parliament under which the new District was constituted stipulated that the District should not become a Parish until the new church was consecrated. Consequently the District remained a part of the parish of All Souls' for ecclesiastical purposes until the consecration of the church on 28 May 1859. The Reverend William Upton Richards, formerly Minister of the Margaret Chapel, was collated and licensed to the Incumbency of All Saints' on 19 October 1849 (the title of Vicar was not assumed until 1868).

The last sermon preached in Margaret Chapel was delivered on 7 April 1850, Low Sunday, by the Reverend C. Marriott, Fellow of Oriel College, Oxford, and the last services were held the next day. Morning Prayer was said at 7 a.m. followed by the Eucharist. The choir of the neighbouring parish church of Saint Andrew's, Wells Street, volunteered to join the Chapel choir in singing the service. Saint Andrew's, Wells Street is a church of which few people have probably heard. It stood on the east side and towards the north end of Wells Street. It was constructed in 1845–47 and became famous for its Catholic tradition introduced 1862–1885 during the incumbency of the Reverend Benjamin Webb. In its prime its musical tradition was as celebrated as that of All Saints', but the fact that the two churches stood only 300 yards apart made the closure of one inevitable. Saint Andrew's was dismantled stone by stone and re-erected in Old Church Lane, Kingsbury, London NW9, in 1934, where it still stands today. The first stone of the new Church of All Saints was laid in a quiet ceremony by Dr Pusey, Regius Professor of Hebrew and Canon of Christ Church in the University of Oxford, on 1 November 1850 at 9.30 a.m. It had been hoped that the construction of the church would take only two years, but lack of finance caused a delay of nearly nine years. Temporary places of worship were found, first in Great Titchfield Street, and after 1855 at 77a Margaret Street.

Through all this upheaval, William Upton Richards pursued a quiet, steady and extensive ministry. The Church probably never quite overcame the opprobrium it had attracted in some degree by the secession of Frederick Oakeley, and Richards and his work were viewed with a measure of suspicion, but nevertheless the work was done. He played an important role in the founding of the Society of All Saints (Sisters of the Poor), hearing the first confession of Harriet Brownlow Byron, the Foundress on 3 July 1848. After this she began to keep a definite rule of life under the supervision of Richards, who encouraged her to read the Fathers of the Church and recommended that she should train as a nurse at King's College Hospital. Eventually she took up residence at 67 Mortimer Street with three incurable invalids and two orphans, and for the first six months she cared for these inmates alone. One room was fitted up as an oratory and on the vigil of St Andrew 1851 Upton Richards celebrated the Eucharist there for the nascent community. For the remainder of his life, the Community was one of his foremost concerns.

His ministry at All Saints' was never easy. Funds were raised with difficulty to build the parochial school which eventually housed 340 children. The school was housed initially in two buildings at 30

Great Castle Street East and 10 Great Titchfield Street. A new site, at 84 Margaret Street, was acquired in 1867, and the total cost of constructing the schools, designed by Butterfield, was £6,137 3s 7½d when the buildings were completed in 1870. Richards contributed £500 himself to the cost of the project. The early finances of the Church are largely a mystery, the first statement of accounts being published only in 1864. The accounts showed a deficit for the year ending 24 December 1863 of £477 15s 2d, and an appeal was launched to clear the debt. This is the first indication of the problems of financing a poorly-endowed inner-city church, a problem which has been something of a recurring nightmare to every succeeding Vicar. There were no pew rents at All Saints', and repeated appeals had to be made to the congregation to clear recurring deficits.

The style of worship was unremarkable by the standards of its later developments. A comparatively small altar (the remains of which can still be seen), adorned by a cross and two candlesticks, with the possible addition of vases of flowers, would have graced the east end. Eucharistic vestments were not introduced until August 1867, and then only after the congregation had been allowed to discuss the matter for the preceding fifteen months. Statues, incense, sanctuary lamps and reservation of the Blessed Sacrament were unknown. To a generation which takes such things for granted such omissions may seem strange, but Richards was fundamentally a Church of England man. He had lived through the great crisis of Oakeley's secession in 1845, and throughout his incumbency, he was repeatedly troubled by the secession of curates and members of the congregation alike. From his memoirs, Oakeley himself was convinced that the only purpose that the Church should serve was that of being a clearing house for those on their way to Rome. But Richards apparently never fell under suspicion either of contemplating secession himself or of directly encouraging it in others. His obituary in the *Church Times* recorded that there was no clergyman in England who laboured more earnestly or more successfully in countering the temptation to secede.[3]

It is not easy to give any estimation of the character of a man about whom so little is known. His contemporaries judged him to be a man of great simplicity and great sincerity, piety, gentleness and tact, famous not so much for marked ability or wide learning as for sheer dogged persistence in carrying out the principles he had learned from those of a greater intellectual capacity than himself. Without wishing to belittle his efforts, it is fair to say that the real influence and ability, as far as fund-raising and construction were concerned, lay with a small group of wealthy laymen in the congregation. His role was to preside over the whole enterprise as a man utterly above any kind of suspicion who found himself thrust into a situation not of his choosing by events over which he had no control, and to fulfil that task with a high sense of duty and responsibility. He was no theologian and he published nothing of great significance. Possibly he might have remained in the Manuscripts Department of the British Museum for the whole of his life, had the events of 1845 not occurred, but he was entrusted with a task, difficult and uncertain though the future was, and he performed it with impeccable dedication and conscientiousness.

The author of an obituary of Richards analysed the secret of his influence as threefold. The first was an unaffected simplicity, both in tastes and in character, as if he had spent the whole of his life in Cornwall. He never adopted that somewhat cosmopolitan and diplomatic air affected by many of the clergy of the capital city, in reflection of the character of those to whom they minister. Secondly, he had a most winning affectionateness which linked him to the catholic movement more by his great friendship for the characters of the men who were prominently associated with it than by any keen intellectual sympathy for their writings and sayings. To the end of his life he retained a great admiration and affection for Newman, and though the secession of a number of his curates caused him great personal distress, it never for one moment shook his own confidence in the Church of England and its essential Catholicity. Thirdly, he was endowed with the great gift of practical wisdom. It was often remarked that he did not keep up with the developments of the aesthetical side of the catholic movement, but his basic simplicity taught him to be wary and sensitive to the point at which ceremonial may lapse imperceptibly into elaborate trifling, or it may obscure the truths which it is intended to express.[4] If he delayed the introduction of eucharistic vestments until 1867, more than twenty-two years after their use had been revived in 1845, then it was because he judged the time to be inopportune rather than because of any fearfulness.

As a preacher, he was described as 'plain but winning, and eminently practical', and as a spiritual adviser, 'most discerning, patient, attentive and kind'. He was a great friend of John Keble, who stayed with him on many occasions, and was much grieved by Keble's death in 1866. In all his dealings and actions he was 'mild, conciliatory and gentlemanlike' and always deeply upset if he sensed any estrangement in his friendships.

William Upton Richards was allowed only ten years of active ministry in the church he had built. Like so many other priests before and after him, the strain of overwork resulted in a series of strokes in November 1869. He remained Vicar for a further three and a half years but took little active role in the parish, though his private ministry to penitents appears to have continued unabated. He preached on only eight occasions in those last few years, the last time being Easter Day 1872, and he celebrated the Eucharist for the last time on 7 July of that year. He lingered on for a further eleven months, dying of a stroke on Monday 16 June 1873 at about 7.35 a.m. at his home, 10 St Andrew's Place, Regent's Park. (Neither he nor his successor lived at the Vicarage, preferring to maintain their own private houses). After a requiem celebration at the church, the body, vested in cassock, surplice and white stole, was buried in Brompton Cemetery on Saturday 21 June. The Eucharist was sung to a setting in F by Richard Redhead, who had been appointed organist of the Margaret Chapel by Frederick Oakeley, as far back as 1839, and the congregation included Fr Mackonochie and Fr Stanton, Gladstone, and the architects Butterfield and Street.

On the Sunday following, 22 June, a sermon was preached by the Reverend G. Body, Rector of Kirkby Mispertown in Yorkshire, and a close friend of Upton Richards, entitled 'The Parting of Elijah and Elisha'. Body was quite certain of where Richards' greatness lay. After making a guarded reference to the secession of Oakeley in 1845, "when the day of trial came and the shepherd forsook his flock", he continued, "Almost alone in this great city he proclaimed Christ's Catholic faith in its integrity, and developed those living sacramental ministries of Christ's Church". Of Richards' total loyalty to the Church of England, he was in no doubt. That part of his sermon which refers to him as a Church of England man "to the very deepest depths of his heart', is an interesting exposition of a Tractarian Catholicism which, constantly plagued by secessions to Rome, endeavoured to assert the full catholicity of the Church of England. Richards' devotion was to a Catholic faith and life, as he believed the English Church to have received them, and not to "an eclectic Catholicism chosen by . . . mere caprice from continental Christianity". His efforts were directed towards giving a living expression to the Catholic features of the Prayer Book, rather than attempting "to engraft on the English Church a system to which she is historically opposed". He was attracted far more by the doctrinal and practical aspects of Catholicism than the external appearance of the liturgy. "To call the sinner to repentence, then to lead him to the feet of Jesus, that he might know the joy of the divine forgiveness . . . was his one great yearning". Body called upon the congregation to remain loyal to the memory of their departed priest, by taking up the mantle of Elijah that had fallen from his shoulders ". . . catching your pastor's spirit, remain in faithful allegiance in that Church in which he lived and died . . . resolve at once to be tenacious in your devotion to Catholic truth, and firm in your allegiance to this English Church".[5]

All Saints' Church has long been accustomed to being staffed by celibate clergy, so the fact that the first four Vicars of the parish were married men may come as something of a surprise. But it should be remembered that clerical celibacy was unusual in 19th century England and there was nothing uncommon about married clergy. It is a sadness that we know nothing of the family of William Upton Richards. Perhaps it is not unreasonable to assume that such a gentle and faithful pastor of souls drew much strength and support from his wife. Caroline Upton Richards died in 1890, and their only unmarried daughter, Madeline, died in November 1896.

Looking back on the life of William Upton Richards, any attempt to describe his life and work more than 110 years after his death is bound to be

Celebration of Holy Communion in Margaret Chapel on the Feast of the Epiphany, 1850

inadequate. He was not a great intellectual and would probably have been the first to admit the fact. He wrote little of any consequence and this assessment of his ministry is based almost entirely on the judicious judgements of his contemporaries. Yet though he has left so little of himself behind, his tenacity and vision ensured the construction of All Saints' Church, and

22

the development of its high and distinctive standard of music and liturgy that continues to this day. Although he was not the architect of the building, the words on the tomb of Sir Christopher Wren in the crypt of St Paul's Cathedral might be borne in mind by the visitor to All Saints' Church: "If you seek a monument, look around you".

One of the most touching tributes to Richards came from the Roman Catholic parish priest of St John's Church, Duncan Terrace, Islington. It is uncertain if Frederick Oakeley ever visited the Chapel or All Saints' Church after his departure in 1845, though he must certainly have passed by it on more than one occasion from sheer curiosity. He bore no ill-will to its Vicar and his ministry and the best indication of his kindness and generosity lies in this tribute that he paid to his successor. "The gentleman who succeeded me . . . and is still its minister, is a person of the most unblemished life, the highest integrity, the most amiable disposition, and the purest intentions; and I have no doubt that good must come of the honest exertions of such a man".[6]

Berdmore Compton, 2nd Vicar, 1873–1886

CHAPTER TWO

THE GENTLEMAN
BERDMORE COMPTON
1873–1886

"His legal training and knowledge, his grasp of principle, and his clear and logical speech, marked him out as a stalwart champion of the good cause."

(The *Church Times*, 10 January 1908)

BERDMORE COMPTON

Born: 14 July 1820
Merton College Oxford 1838–1841
Fellow of Merton College 1841–1851
Assistant Master, Rugby School 1851–1857
Deacon 1853 (Oxford)   Priest 1857 (Worcester)
Rector of Barford 1857–1865
Rector of St. Paul's, Covent Garden 1865–1873
Vicar of All Saints', Margaret Street 1873–1886
Prebendary of Caddington Minor,
St Paul's Cathedral 1897–1908
Died: 3 January 1908

NOT surprisingly, a period of much anxiety and suspense followed the death of William Upton Richards. A vacancy of four months followed before the appointment of his successor. It appears that the interregnum was used by the Roman Catholics as an opportunity to increase their proselytising activities. One of the curates at that time later recalled that frequently he had to counteract the efforts of the Roman clergy who tried to win over members of the congregation. The Romans seemed to believe that the congregation only remained in the Church of England from a personal loyalty to Upton Richards, and that with his death they would leave this 'half-way' house and find their true spiritual home within the Church of Rome. However, they reckoned without the tenacity and faithfulness of the congregation to the teaching of their late Vicar, and, from a congregation of several hundred, six at most were received into the Roman Catholic Church.

Of far greater concern to the congregation was the question of who would succeed their late Vicar. It was rumoured that the Bishop of London (John Jackson, Bishop 1869–1885) was attempting to impose conditions on those to whom he offered the benefice. This was the ideal opportunity to appoint a man who would, while caring for the spiritual needs of the congregation, bring the Church back into Anglican orthodoxy as far as its ritualistic practices were concerned. The *Church Times* printed a list of names of the priests to whom the parish had been offered on conditions that they observed the Purchas Judgement of 1871, namely that eucharistic vestments, the east-ward position, the mixed chalice and wafer bread were illegal. Although the *Church Times* subsequently suggested that the appointment of a Low Church-man was being considered – to extinguish the peculiarity and distinctiveness of All Saints' – it seems unlikely that Bishop Jackson would ever have

seriously considered such a course of action. Whatever views he may have held about the church and its
practices, Bishop Jackson was not the kind of man
who would ignore the wishes and sensitivities of a
particular congregation. He certainly offered the
living to Canon William Walsham How (1823–1897),
chaplain of the English Church in Rome and later first
Bishop of Wakefield (1888–1897). Jackson's offer to
Walsham How imposed the condition that he would
maintain the services of the church in their beauty
'within the allowed limits of the Anglican ritual'; that
he would be a ready and experienced counsellor
'without encouraging (as I fear has been done there of
late) the enervating habit of confession; and who will
introduce a somewhat more evangelical (I am not
using the word in its party sense) and experimental
tone of preaching than has been the ordinary tone
there. That this will satisfy all the congregation I do
not expect. No one whom I could consciously place
there would. But it would satisfy many, and what is
more it would benefit them'. The Bishop then fulmin-
ated against the Church newspapers who had 'amused
themselves and their readers by filling up the benefice
from time to time out of their own imagination'.
Walsham How declined the benefice without hesitation: 'I am too much out of harmony with the whole
system there to be able to work there happily or
usefully'.[1] In 1879 he was appointed suffragan bishop
for East London with the title Bishop of Bedford, and
is remembered for his dynamic work on behalf of the
poor in the East End of London. He is probably best
known as the author of the hymn, 'For all the saints,
who from their labours rest'.

By the end of September, with no appointment
made, the congregation addressed a petition to the
Bishop urging him 'to take into your deep and earnest
consideration our present state of painful anxiety
with regard to the future prospects of this church and

its various works. And we submit that in making the appointment of a new Vicar, the principles of those who have so munificently supported this church through a quarter of a century, have a very strong claim to be regarded and respected, and that if they be so, we doubt not that this great work will be carried on as vigorously and successfully as heretofore'.[2] The petition was signed by some 850 members of the congregation. Whatever he may have thought, the Bishop offered the living without condition on 21 October to the Reverend Berdmore Compton, who was inducted on 28 October 1873.

Berdmore Compton was born on 14 July 1820, the third son of Henry Combe Compton and his wife Charlotte, the daughter of William Mills, of Bisterne, Hampshire. A moderately prosperous and successful politician, Henry Compton was MP for South Hampshire (1835–1857). The family divided their time between their London home in Marylebone and their country house, Minstead Manor at Lyndhurst in Hampshire. We know nothing of Compton's early life except that he was brought up as an evangelical. He was called to the Bar at Lincoln's Inn on 6 June 1843 at the age of twenty-three, but to what extent he practised law, if at all, is uncertain. He was an undergraduate at Merton College, Oxford 1838–1841, graduating 3rd class Literae Humaniores and 1st class in Mathematics. He was elected a Fellow of Merton in 1841 and remained so until after his appointment as an Assistant Master at Rugby School in 1851 when, on his marriage to Agnes Priscilla, fifth daughter of Andrew Mortimer Drummond, he relinquished his Fellowship. The headmaster of Rugby at the time was Edward Meyrick Goulburn (1818–1897), a priest of conservative tradition whose dislike of the liberal positions of his predecessors, Arnold and Tait, led to a decline in the numbers at the school and his own resignation in 1857. Goulburn became Vicar of St

John's, Paddington in 1859 before moving to be Dean of Norwich in 1866 where he remained until his death. Compton was much influenced by Goulburn and gradually relinquished his earlier evangelical views in favour of a more strict ecclesiastical orthodoxy. He was ordained deacon in 1853 by Bishop Samuel Wilberforce of Oxford 'who always had the highest regard for him' on the strength of his mastership at Rugby, that being considered to be sufficient title. Goulburn resigned from Rugby in 1857 and Compton left in the same year, possibly in sympathy. He never lost his admiration and affection for Goulburn, and, after the latter's death, published a glowing memoir of him in 1899.

He was ordained priest in 1857 by Bishop Henry Pepys of Worcester, who nominated him to the living of Barford, a beautiful village close to Warwick, where he remained for eight years. It may seem rather inadequate to remark that nothing of note happened during these years but such was the case. Compton probably led the quiet and tranquil life of a country parson in mid-Victorian England, with few if any worries. He was certainly not without friends and influence because, in 1865, he was nominated by the Duke of Bedford to the comparatively lucrative living of St Paul's, Covent Garden, a Low Church parish. He stayed there for eight years transforming the Church into 'a place of meeting for earnest men of all schools of thought'.[3] He became a close friend of the Dean of St. Paul's Cathedral and Bishop Wilkinson 'in whose penitentiary work at St Peter's, Great Windmill Street, he was warmly interested'.[4] It was Wilkinson who brought Compton to the attention of Bishop Jackson of London and suggested that he be transferred to All Saints'.

Compton's appointment to All Saints' was received with undisguised pleasure and relief by the congregation and the friends and supporters of the work of the church. The *Guardian* reported that the congregation had been given 'great satisfaction' by the news of the appointment, and the *Church Times* of 24 October wished Mr Compton 'all prosperity in his new sphere of duty, and we thankfully accept this answer to the fervent utterances of the congregation of All Saints' and other churchmen throughout the country. The Bishop of London deserves a word of commendation for having thus solved a somewhat difficult problem'. Not all were overjoyed at the appointment. The evangelical movement viewed it with dismay and *The Rock* deplored it as one of the greatest blows struck at the Church of England, expressing disappointment that such an injury should have been inflicted upon her by one of her own bishops. The induction was set for 28 October, only seven days after the appointment, to ensure that the congregation should have the pleasure of hearing their new Vicar preach to them on All Saints' Day.

The appointment put to an end all worries and fears that Bishop Jackson might be planning to suppress or substantially alter the Tractarian nature of the worship at All Saints'. But apparently there was a fascinating contingency plan which would have been put into effect should the bishop have got his own way in making serious changes at All Saints'. The Prime Minister of the day was the great William Gladstone, who had remained a friend and supporter of the work and witness of the church since he had first formed an attachment to the Margaret Chapel during Frederick Oakeley's ministry. The living of St Peter's Church, Vere Street (now a daughter church of All Souls', Langham Place), had recently fallen vacant and the patronage of the Church lay with the Crown, exercised on its behalf by the Prime Minister. Gladstone, after discussion with prominent members of the congregation of All Saints', decided to keep the living of St Peter's vacant, pending the appointment

31

of a new Vicar to All Saints'. Should the Bishop succeed in his presumed intention of changing the nature of All Saints' beyond all recognition by making an unsympathetic appointment, Gladstone would appoint the Reverend C. H. Christie, senior assistant curate of All Saints' as the new Vicar of St. Peter's, on the understanding that he would take the entire congregation of All Saints' with him to continue its work in another building. As matters turned out, there was no need to put the plan into effect, but one cannot help but wonder how the congregation of St Peter's would have viewed such an arrangement.[5]

Berdmore Compton made it quite clear that he would not be a party to any measures aimed at transforming All Saints' into anything other than it had been under Upton Richards, and during his thirteen-year incumbency both music and ceremonial flourished under his direction. By 'his gentle nature and great power of sympathy'[6] he succeeded in winning the support and affection of the congregation who perhaps did not appreciate everything that he did. In his sermon on All Saints' Day, the new Vicar 'spoke strongly on the point of keeping up the services as a standard and typical pattern of a refined and devout parochial service; declaring himself very slow to make changes . . . He claimed for the ideal of divine service as conducted at All Saints' less ornateness than solemnity'.[7] Compton appears to have pursued a wisely cautious policy during his incumbency, making as few changes as possible. He was in the unenviable situation of running a flourishing church which was, nevertheless, in some financial difficulty, and he was following a popular and much-loved incumbent. His wise policy of consolidation was well summed up in a sermon delivered at St Paul's Church, Knightsbridge in 1888, two years after leaving All Saints'. 'The second incumbent of a recently-constituted cure of souls has always a peculiar sphere of duty . . . His aim is as far as possible to eliminate the personal element from the system, so that the parochial machinery may acquire such habitual steadiness and smoothness of action, that it shall . . . be independent of the personal influence of the incumbent for the time being. The second incumbent has to use the reins and bit, rather than the whip . . . His aim will be to take advantage of the existing system of services and ritual, rather than to alter and improve them. He can, as the pioneer cannot, press on to perfection, safely devote his entire energy to teaching the baptised to live the regenerate life which they have received in the sacrament of baptism, the communicant to rise higher and higher as that life is again and again renewed by the sacrament of the Eucharist.[8]

There was no formal parish paper during the years of Compton's incumbency, so it is not easy to decide on the directions in which he used the 'reins and bit'. The first change was the severing of links between the All Saints' Sisters and the parish. The Sisterhood had been the brainchild of Upton Richards and was regarded very much as a parochial institution. Richards had acted as Chaplain to the community and inevitably he bound the parish and the community together. Now he was gone and there was no need for his successor as Vicar to succeed him as Chaplain. Whether the decision was made by Mother Harriet, the Foundress, or by Berdmore Compton himself is uncertain. It is possible that Compton may have felt it wise not to attempt to fulfil the unique and distinctive role played by Upton Richards in this respect, or he may have felt that he was insufficiently qualified to minister to the spiritual needs of the community. Whatever the reason, the Sisters chose as their new Chaplain the Reverend Father Richard Benson, Founder and Superior of the

33

Society of St John the Evangelist, at Oxford.

In 1880 and 1881, Compton presided at a conference of experienced priests and liturgical scholars called in response to the expressed anxiety of those who were worried about the increasing diversity of ritual practised by those who professed to be aiming at the maintenance of Catholic doctrine and usage in the Church of England. 'In some cases the advances of fancy-ritual were so distracting that the profane were tempted to the conclusion that each church was trying to outbid its neighbour in such spectacular effects or unaccustomed ceremonies, as should mark it out for distinction in the public mind. We fear that in the next decade the evil attained to even larger dimensions'.[9] The conference met on forty-eight occasions between January 1880 and July 1881, and produced a commentary on the rubrics of the Prayer Book entitled *Ritual Conformity*. The book went to a second edition in 1882 but it is doubtful if it was ever widely followed. The ritual movement was proceeding at a pace too fast to be constrained, and furthermore the book, although 'marked by much wisdom and commonsense as well as scholarship', was 'much hindered by the decisive view promulgated in favour of the Sarum sequence of colours of the vestments'.[10]

The year 1883 saw the fiftieth anniversary of Keble's Assize Sermon, regarded by Newman as the beginning of the Oxford Movement, and Compton took great care to mark the event. He preached a sermon, spread over three Sundays in November entitled 'The Fiftieth Year of the Reformation of the Nineteenth Century'. The sermon, in which he outlined the principles of the movement, is an interesting insight into Compton's views on the Catholicity of the Church of England. He begins with a reproachful reference to John Henry Newman, 'the great English Cardinal of the Italian Church' who was 'great in the honour of men, but greater perhaps he might have been, in no honour of men, in abiding patiently wherein he was called'. Comparing him with Sidney Faithorn Green, the Vicar of Miles Platting in Lancashire, who was imprisoned for disobeying the judgements of the court set up under the Public Worship Regulation Act, Compton remarked that Newman would have been held in high honour were he in a similar position 'reviled by church dignitaries, persecuted and imprisoned as an English priest in Lancaster gaol, and all manner of evil said against him for Christ's sake'.

Compton believed that dogma was the fundamental principle of the Oxford Movement and that the dogmas of the church should be verified from Holy Scripture, though in this matter 'our reformation has as yet made but little progress . . . At present every crude opinion to be found in a Latin dress . . . is hastily accepted and confidently quoted as a dogma of the Catholic Church'. Compton held that the Church existed as a body or corporation and that this had been long obscured. It was a spiritual reality, the life of which was visible in every true branch of the Church. Newman had conceived this to exist in triplicate – Latin, Greek and Anglican, distinguishable from each other only by secondary, fortuitious, and local, though important, characteristics. 'Of course the great theologian can no longer hold this theory, since he has repudiated any Church but the visible Roman Church. Nor indeed . . . can we so minimize Roman error, as to accept this theory throughout, while Rome remains what she is at present . . . the irreformable Church of Italy'. He dismissed the much-loved phrase 'Western Church' as 'a branch which never has existed . . . and is historically a mere object of Papal ambition, and a synonym for the Roman Church'. Though he swiped constantly at the Roman Church because of its 'error', he was also highly critical of the Via Media theory, at one time much vaunted by Newman, of the Church of England. It was 'true, as a statement of fact, and possibly a sound principle in secular politics, but ruinous as a motive or principle, of religious action'. Popular manuals of devotion borrowed from the Roman Church were equally anathema with their 'red edges, uncouth Albert Durer engravings, or photographs of modern French pictures, the effusions of later mediaeval authors or the gushing sentimentality of continental religionists'. Conscious of the fact that he was speaking on the fiftieth anniversary of Keble's Sermon, he reiterated the latter's charge of National Apostasy, called for the spiritual independence of the Church and sharply criticised the tendency for secular authorities to interfere in 'that which hath not been entrusted to them . . . Any utterances of theirs, claiming direction of spiritual ways are . . . dangerously near to downright usurpation of the Authority of the Holy Ghost'. As Keble had sounded against the Church Temporalities (Ireland) Act in 1833, Compton railed against the Public Worship Regulation Act and 'the imprisonment of God's witness'.[11]

Berdmore Compton proved himself a worthy successor to Upton Richards in that he was Anglican to the core and, for all the fact that he was Vicar of a church that was by popular Anglican standards close to Roman Catholicism in its practices, never once considered leaving the Church of his birth and training. Like his predecessor, he also had a healthy attitude to matters of ceremonial. 'It is wrong for us, who plainly repudiate the uncatholic error of Roman peculiarities in doctrine and discipline . . . to set forth a subserviency to Roman authority, by a servile imitation of Roman peculiarities in details of worship. Let us be outwardly, what we are inwardly, English in our Catholicity, not Italian or Belgian'.

There is something of an early Tractarian in this strong emphasis on the Englishness of the Catholic Church in England (i.e. the Church of England). Begun by Upton Richards, it has continued as a major theme in the life and witness of All Saints' Church, and of successive Vicars. Perhaps one of its greatest strengths has been this very point. Though it was many decades before a Bishop of London was to feel entirely happy with the un-Anglican liturgical practices of this Catholic conventicle in the centre of his diocese, its loyalty to the Church of England has never been in real doubt, and its incumbents have always been above the suspicion of looking longingly and wistfully in the direction of the Vatican.

As with his firm commitment to the Catholic faith as he believed the Church of England to have received and interpreted it, so he shared Upton Richards' belief that it was the duty of all Christians to take good care of their personal lives so as to be seen to be efficient witnesses to the renewal of life brought about by faith and trust in God. 'Our ranks are cumbered with worse than inefficient combatants, whose spiritual life goes on from bad to worse, ruining their own salvation, and giving occasion to the enemy to harden themselves against the truth . . . As long as Faith was subjective and hazy and men . . . trimmed it, irrespective of dogma to any shape that pleased themselves, the camp of Faith might contain many who had not a living faith. But when the sifting comes . . . and the border line of a dogmatic and objective faith becomes sharp and clear, then unbelievers see and feel that they do not believe . . .'.[12] Compton was quite set in his own mind that there was such a thing as a non-Roman, Catholic faith, and that it could be maintained with integrity against Romanists, Rationalists and Evangelicals.

Although Compton did his best with the conference of 1880–1881 to secure some kind of generally accepted degree of liturgical uniformity and was highly critical of those churches which adopted what he described as 'fancy ritual', he was acutely aware of the importance of ceremonial in its entirety and saw no sense in discontinuing those actions which might be deemed inessential. While it was perfectly possible to whittle away those actions, such as reducing the Eucharist to the Oblation of the Elements, the recitation of the words of Institution, and the administration of the consecrated species to the people, then 'the slightest failure invalidates the entire act'. Modern liturgical scholars might disagree with Compton's assumption that the Eucharist might be reduced to such a minimum and still remain a Eucharist, but his point is made. He was proud of the ritual progress of the Oxford Movement, though suspicious of mere imitation of Roman practices, and would not allow any diminution in the liturgical tradition of All Saints'. The Church which gives up these things, which cuts off its stately fringes thread by thread, will gradually sink down to the ragged surplices and threadbare gown of our own early days . . . You must take care of the fringes, and then you may have grace given you to preserve inviolate the central fabric'.[13]

Towards the end of his incumbency, Compton was faced with the problem that has faced every Vicar since the Church was built – the constant need of raising funds to maintain the building and its work. The dirt of London in the 1880s, aggravated by soot from the gaslights and unchecked by the Clean Air Act and other modern conveniences such as electric light, was causing major problems to the interior of the Church less than 30 years after its completion. The interior needed a thorough cleaning, and especially the frescoes by William Dyce (1806–1864) on the east wall which were 'in a sad state of dirt, if not worse'.[14] An appeal for £400 raised £535 4s 6d and was spent on cleaning, redecorating, renovating and repolishing the fabric and fittings. (For some reason that is not immediately clear, it was decided not to attempt any work on the frescoes.)

In 1886, the thorough cleaning of the Church completed, and the great festivals of Christmas and Easter past, Compton felt that his ministry at All Saints' was at an end and he submitted his resignation to the Bishop on 3 May, the day after Low Sunday. He had reached the now customary, but then unusual, retiring age of sixty-five. He continued as Vicar until 27 July, and the remaining weeks of his incumbency saw one of his greatest achievements – Edward White Benson, Archbishop of Canterbury, preaching in All Saints' on Ascension Day, 3 June 1886.

Compton's life then took a rather unusual turn in that for the remainder of his life he held no further stipendiary post in the Church of England. Most of his time was spent in administering his estate in Warwickshire and playing the role of the country squire. He enjoys the distinction of being the only Vicar of All Saints' to have ranked, personally, among the landed gentry of England, for in 1872 he had inherited Atherstone Hall in Warwickshire from a distant cousin, Charles Holt Bracebridge. Atherstone was an early eighteenth century house of six bays and three storeys to which a ballroom was added at the end of the century. At the beginning of the nineteenth century, lower three-bay additions were built at either side of the original building and the whole structure was rendered. On 18 May 1908 his son James (1859–1937) assumed the additional surname of Bracebridge by Royal Licence, and the Compton-Bracebridge family remained at Atherstone until the middle of the twentieth century. The house was demolished in 1963.

Compton did not entirely sever his work with the

Church, being an active member of the Standing Committees of both the Society for Promoting Christian Knowledge and the Society for the Propagation of the Gospel, and in 1897 he was appointed to the prebendal stall of Caddington Minor in St Paul's Cathedral. He valued the appointment as bringing him into closer connection with the diocese in which he had served for twenty-one years and also with his old friend Robert Gregory (1819–1911), the Dean of St Paul's. In its obituary, the *Church Times* described him as 'an excellent platform speaker' whose speech at the great meeting of the English Church Union in 1874 to protest against the Public Worship Regulation Act 'is a pleasant memory to many'. He shared the platform with such giants as Pusey and Liddon but made a great impression. 'His legal training and knowledge, his grasp of principle, and his clear and logical speech, marked him out as a stalwart champion of the good cause'. Thirty years later, in 1904, then eighty-four years old, he made another great speech at an ECU meeting in defence of the Athanasian Creed. 'This is well-remembered for the clearness and vigour with which the revered old man put his case for the truth'. Compton had in fact resigned from the ECU at the time of the *Lux Mundi* controversy in 1889, being an old-fashioned theologian who had 'scant sympathy with refinements and speculations. In his later years he regretted the step and took to praising the society, declaring his belief that God had raised it up to save the Church of England'.

During his time at St Paul's, Covent Garden, he turned that church into something of an intellectual debating centre and probably would have been singled out for preferment had he not accepted the living of All Saints' in 1873. Towards the end of his life he was asked why he had thrown in his lot with the hated and despised ritualists; he replied simply,

'Because they were unjustly treated'. He had studied the Mackonochie case and came to the conclusion 'that everything the Judicial Committee of the Privy Council said was wrong was right, and everything they declared to be right was clearly wrong'.[15] When the Royal Commission on Ecclesiastical Discipline began its sittings in 1904 many thought that Compton would make an admirable witness as a critic of the Ridsdale Judgement of 1877 in which the Privy Council had declared the wearing of Eucharistic vestments to be illegal. Compton initially accepted but later withdrew his consent, saying that he 'could not trust himself to speak with calmness of the majority of the Committee who decided the case'.[16]

Compton rarely visited All Saints' after his departure, giving his successor, William Whitworth, scope to run the parish in his own way. When he stayed at his London house, 55 Pont Street, he attended St Paul's, Knightsbridge, occasionally reading the lessons. His wife, Agnes, died on 13 November 1902. Compton lived to a great age, surviving Whitworth, and walking in the procession at

Atherstone Hall, Warwickshire, country seat of Berdmore Compton

the induction of the his successor, George Holden, in 1905. He died in January 1908 of renal failure, in his eighty-eighth year, barely two months before Holden. His funeral took place at Atherstone on 8 January, conducted by his nephew, the Reverend Charles Compton, Rector of Minstead, and the Reverend W. Nothcott, Vicar of Atherstone. Memorial services were held the same day at All Saints' and at St Paul's Cathedral. *The Times'* obituary referred to him as a man 'of stately comeliness, of wide knowledge, and great charm of manner'. But perhaps the best indication of what Compton surrendered in accepting the living of All Saints' is contained in the following letter of Bishop Samuel Wilberforce who wrote of him while he was still at Covent Garden, 'Compton is a man who singularly fascinates you. His intense earnestness and devotion, his great humility, his commonsense, his savoire faire, would all tend to make him an excellent Bishop. I must call Gladstone's attention to him'.[17]

CHAPTER THREE

THE MISSIONARY
WILLIAM WHITWORTH
1886–1905

*"I can only resolve . . . patiently
to do my best, trusting to your generous
forbearance towards my shortcomings
and deficiencies"*

(William Allen Whitworth writing in the 'Parish
Paper' for 21 November 1886.)

William Allen Whitworth (seated centre), 3rd Vicar, 1886–1905, surrounded by his curates, in 1890. Standing on the far left is Henry Mackay who became the 5th Vicar of All Saints' in 1908

WILLIAM ALLEN WHITWORTH

Born: 1 February 1840

St John's College, Cambridge 1858–1862

(Fellow of St John's College 1867–1885)

Professor of Mathematics, Queen's College,
Liverpool 1862–1864

Deacon 1865   Priest 1866

Curate of St Anne's, Birkenhead 1865

Curate of St Luke's, Liverpool 1866–1870

Priest in Charge of Christ Church, Liverpool
1870–1875

Vicar of St John the Evangelist, Hammersmith
1875–1886

Rector of Aberdaron with Llanfaelrhys 1885–1905

Vicar of All Saints', Margaret Street 1886–1905

Prebendary of Caddington Major,
St Paul's Cathedral 1900–1905

Died: 12 March 1905

AGAIN there was a long gap between incumbents; on this occasion some six months elapsed between the resignation of Mr Compton and the appointment of his successor, the Reverend William Allen Whitworth. During that time it was inevitable that there should be some recurrence of anxiety for the future among longer serving members of the congregation who could remember the episcopal machinations preceding the appointment of Berdmore Compton. There was an unspoken fear on the part of some that Frederick Temple, the new Bishop of London, would seek to impose a subservient priest who would attempt to curb the outward expression of their Catholic convictions. In such a period of uncertainty, it comes as no surprise to find that the Church had begun to drift further into debt. All Saints' had an endowment of only £150 and was heavily dependent on the voluntary giving of the congregation, and there was a danger 'lest they should be tempted to withhold their offerings, when they have no security but that an incumbent may be appointed who may ignore their cherished convictions and inaugurate some new system'.[1] By the beginning of November, the church was in debt to the sum of £400 and the churchwardens felt obliged to inform the new Vicar of the fact. However, at the same time, they were determined that the new Vicar should not start his ministry with such financial worries and they launched an appeal which raised £404 16s, enabling them to hand over a church in surplus to the sum of £20!

The Reverend William Whitworth was collated to the benefice on 4 November and inducted by the Archdeacon of Middlesex on 11 November 1886. William Whitworth was born on 1 February 1840, the eldest son of the Reverend William Whitworth, a schoolmaster of Runcorn, Cheshire, and his wife Susanna, daughter of George Coyne of Kilbeggan,

Co. Westmeath. He was educated at Sandicroft School in Norwich and at St John's College, Cambridge, where he was in residence from 1858 to 1862. He read Mathematics, graduating as 16th Wrangler, and proved to be a scholar of original ability in that field. He was elected a Fellow of the College in 1867, remaining so until his marriage in 1885. Though his name is not immediately familiar today, he was a mathematician of some competence, publishing six books in that field including *Choice and Chance, Exercises in Algebra, Modern Analytical Geometry, Trilinear Coordinates*, etc. After graduating in 1862, he taught for two years as Professor of Mathematics at Queen's College in Liverpool. 'His lucidity and simpleness of exposition, the directness and obviousness of his proofs, belong to a mathematical perception of a very high order'.[2]

Although Whitworth immersed himself in his work at All Saints', he did not entirely lose contact with his former profession, publishing various works from time to time.

It was at Liverpool that he took decisive steps on the road to his eventual profession by seeking ordination from William Jacobson, Bishop of Chester. Beyond the bald statement that he was ordained deacon in 1865 and priest in 1866, we know nothing about the germination and development of his vocation during those years at Liverpool. His first curacy was at the Church of St Anne, Birkenhead, where he stayed for only a short time before moving to St Luke's, Liverpool in 1866. He spent five years as Priest in Charge of Christ Church, Liverpool and moved to London in 1875. While at Liverpool he became a friend of E. H. McNeil, a leading evangelical figure among the clergy of that city, known for his great sincerity and independence. 'The two joined in a refusal to bow before majorities, or to oppress holders of unpopular opinions'.[3] In his later years Whitworth was known as a person of impetuosity and resolution, both perhaps initiated by his friendship with McNeil. He was prominently connected with the work of the Parochial Missions and this probably brought about his move to London in 1875. He was appointed Vicar of St John the Evangelist, Hammersmith, a Butterfield church constructed in 1858–9 and described as one of his 'less costly churches'. Whitworth made a big impression on the church. 'His strenuous character, ready resources and dauntless energy found full scope'. He added a tower to St John's in 1881–2, erected a large mission hall, enlarged the church schools, laid the plans and foundations for the construction of another church, Holy Innocents, Paddenswick Road (completed in 1890). But above all, he maintained a work of spiritual and pastoral care, especially among the young, which quickly marked the church as 'one of the centres of Catholic power and worship in the west of London'. Whitworth was clearly a person of great vision and imagination, though inclined to be impetuous, and it was probably these qualities that marked him out in the eyes of Bishop Temple as the ideal candidate for All Saints', Margaret Street. Berdmore Compton effectively enabled his successor to innovate and develop in a way that he could not. As the immediate successor of Upton Richards, the founder and pioneer, his role was to consolidate. To introduce change would have been disastrous and that was neither his role nor desire. By doing almost everything that Upton Richards had done, almost in the same way, he had ensured that his successor would have much greater freedom of action and be able to make changes with less hostility than that which might have greeted his own efforts.

Whitworth was, at first, somewhat reluctant to accept the living. He had no musical talent and very small private means, and All Saints' was famed for the beauty of its music and for the poverty of its endowment. The further question of his residence also raised some difficulty. Both Upton Richards and Berdmore Compton had lived in their own private houses and left the occupation of the clergy house to the curates and the choir. But Whitworth felt that if he lived other than on the site, he would never be in full control. The churchwardens replied that he would find the building very inconvenient, but they made no objection to his plan to live there with his family, moving the choir and one of the clergy to No. 8 Margaret Street, and finding accommodation for the others close by, and continuing the collegiate system of common meals in the refectory.

There is a curious story relating to Whitworth's financial means which were quite limited, unlike those of Upton Richards and Berdmore Compton. In June 1885, while still at Hammersmith, he married Sarah Louisa Whitworth, only daughter of Timms Harvey Elwes of Ipswich. In accordance with College policy, he was obliged to resign his Fellowship at St John's but, in return, the College presented him to one of the livings in its gift, and he became Rector of Aberdaron with Llanfaelrhys two remote hamlets on the Lleyn Peninsula in North Wales. The living was a sinecure in the truest sense of the word, there being a resident vicar who cared for the parishes. But Whitworth was not the sort of person to regard even a small sinecure as income without responsibility and he handed over half his share to an adjacent Welsh parish, and the remainder he kept to spend on other church purposes.

The early months of his incumbency at All Saints' were not easy for reasons which, at this distance, are now impossible to discern. It appears that Whitworth aroused some annoyance in the conservative and traditional congregation. Four years after his arrival, he published *Quam Dilecta*, a

49

history of the church from its misty origins as Margaret Chapel until his own day. It included the following, relating to his arrival as Vicar: 'By his impetuosity he aroused an opposition, which formulated the charge that he was violating the intentions of the founders. Misunderstandings followed which may well be forgotten. One thing . . . ought not to be forgotten . . . the characteristic generosity of the Bishop, who threw himself into the breach and assumed the responsibility of the changes that were being made, drawing down upon his own strong shoulders much of the resentment which was at first directed towards the Vicar'.[4]

With the arrival of William Whitworth as third Vicar, we begin to know much more about the day-to-day work of the Church and the thoughts of its Vicars. One of Whitworth's first acts was to dispense with *Home Words* which had functioned as the parish magazine and three hundred copies of which were circulated monthly: 'Inside the cover were advertisements about groceries, books, spectacles, teething powders, printing, etc. etc. . . . I considered the matter and prayed over it . . . the Lord led me clearly. He did not want me as His ambassador to be an advertising medium for soap and soda, for chemicals and boots. I gave it up as soon as possible. The whole thing went'.[5] No copies of the much despised *Home Words* appear to have survived in the parish archives, but we are inclined to accept Whitworth's statement as implying that it contained little, if anything, concerning the life of the parish. The Parish Paper that he introduced is, essentially, that which is still published.

In his first public letter addressed to the parish, Whitworth reassured the congregation that he accepted the particular and peculiar mission of All Saints' as being that of providing services to set forth the dignity, the grandeur and glory and the beauty of

Christian worship – 'not as a spectacle, nor as a performance, but – in such a way as shall always conduce to devotion and help the worship of the heart'. At the same time he delivered something of a bombshell to the financially straitened parish by telling them that he would scarcely expect the blessing of God upon their offerings unless a tenth were given away 'in unselfish charity to objects external to our own church and parish'. Modestly, he admitted that he did not have the talents of Berdmore Compton and that it would be a long time before he came near to filling the position that Compton had filled in the life of the parish and its people. 'I can only resolve . . . patiently to do my best, trusting to your generous forbearance towards my shortcomings and deficiencies'.[6]

The first issue of the Parish Paper, for January 1887, contained his worries about the spirituality of the church. All Saints' was constantly being visited by people, very few of whom used it as a place of prayer, and when strangers visited the church 'there is rarely presented to them that practical monition to devotion which would be strongly impressed upon them if they saw others using the place for spiritual purposes. He proposed to arrange a rota 'of devout persons' who would use the church hour by hour for spiritual reading and prayer. He urged members of the congregation, even the most busy, to set aside an hour of quiet during the week for meditation, self-examination, and prayers 'other than those they offer daily – morning and night'. The congregation were told that they needed to practise the art of hearing sermons, to regard the hearing of sermons as a sacred duty, and to find grace in listening even to a bad sermon![7] The Cycle of Prayer was initiated, but owing to the small response, it was limited to Wednesdays and Fridays only.

The inevitable problem of finance reared up in

the issue for February and we are given some figures to show how much anxiety the matter caused to successive Vicars and Churchwardens. The church accounts showed bad deficits at the end of the five preceding years: 1881 2s 3d; 1882 – £69 13s 5d; 1883 – £316 18s 10d; 1884 – £111 17s 11d; 1885 – £87 16s 6d. Whitworth warned the parish that steps would need to be taken to establish the church finances on a sounder footing. Either expenditure would have to be brought down, or income would need to be increased. The new Vicar was still dissatisfied by the meagre support given to foreign mission.

The Parish Paper also gives us an idea of the Sunday schedule of services. Benediction of course was completely unknown. The word 'Mass' was absolute anathema, and the clergy were never addressed as 'Father'. The picture reveals a very full schedule indeed:

7.00 am	Celebration
8.00 am	Celebration
9.00 am	Celebration
10.30 am	Mattins and Sermon
11.45 am	High Celebration
3.30 pm	Litany
4.00 pm	Evensong
4.50 pm	Instruction
5.45 pm	Mens' Service and Sermon
7.00 pm	Evensong and Sermon

Lent 1887 gave Whitworth his first real opportunity actively to begin his desired objective of deepening individual spirituality. He urged the congregation to a three-fold Lenten discipline. Firstly, they should deepen their sorrow for sin, by self-denial, almsgiving, self-examination and confession. Secondly, they should seek to increase their spiritual knowledge by some special study and 'receive instruction in the deeper mysteries of the faith.

The want of knowledge makes meditation almost impossible for some. They do not know the facts on which they ought to meditate'. Thirdly, he called them to endeavour to seek 'a closer communion with God' by frequent attendance at the altar and an eager anticipation of the Easter Communion. 'The Easter Communion is to be received in the light with which our souls have been illuminated in Lent, and it is to be a new consecration of our lives to be lived in fellowship with Christ'.[8]

Evidently Lent was something of a success, for the Vicar was able to write in the Parish Paper for April, 'It is not too soon to thank God for the large and attentive congregations that have crowded the church on Thursday mornings and Tuesday afternoons'. The Lenten discipline for 1888 proved to be even more demanding with a requirement that members of the congregation should read a book of the New Testament through from the beginning to the end 'with the aid of such notes and helps as are at your disposal'; read a commentary on the gospels 'carefully verifying the references to the Holy Scripture'; read a book 'of solid theological teaching as distinguished from meditations and reflections'; read writings in defence and explanation of doctrines that you hold 'which are attacked in articles you may read'; and finally, 'listen to sermons regularly and patiently, not only when some eloquent preacher compels your attention . . . We cannot be forever chewing the cud of our childish knowledge. If we try to sustain ourselves on what we learnt as children, it is no wonder that our interest flags and our hearts grow cold'.[9]

Whitworth believed that All Saints' had three distinct objectives. Firstly, to offer a model of liturgical beauty in beautiful surroundings, as an example of 'unswerving loyalty to the Church of England and of minute attentions to the directions of the Prayer Book'. Like his two predecessors, he was firmly a 'Church of England man' and he would have no sympathy for those who experimented with liturgies and doctrines other than those to be found in the Book of Common Prayer. Secondly, Whitworth believed that the church of All Saints', well-staffed as it was, had a duty to maintain itself as a centre of spiritual ministration where priests should always be available and ready to help any who sought advice or counsel of any description. The third objective was, superficially, no more than would be required of any church – that it should be a centre of missionary activity – but Whitworth envisaged an unusual and rather major enterprise, which had nothing to do with the geographical parish of All Saints'.

The parish of All Saints' had never been very large, consisting of only a few streets. Its population was diminishing and the opportunities for local parochial work were increasingly limited. There were six clergy on the staff and, while this was certainly not in excess of what was required for the frequent services in the church, 'there seemed to be a want of proportion in the work as long as the opportunities for pastoral visitation were so few'. There was little basic pastoral work that could be done as training, for example, by a newly ordained deacon, and no work to be done by the congregation since all the visiting in the parish was done under the direction of the Sisters by their community.

Evaluating the situation, Whitworth decided that the clergy had 'time to spare in the afternoons and evenings, which is not required for work in our little parish', and that there was 'a large number of ladies who are able and willing to visit the poor, to conduct meetings and classes for them . . .'.[10] He envisaged that mission work might be undertaken in the name of All Saints' in large parishes in the poorer parts of London. The Vicar of such a parish would give up to All Saints' a defined section of his cure, with the use of a mission chapel or hall for Sunday evening services. He would not in any way control or direct the work, though he would have the right to terminate it absolutely if he was at all dissatisfied with it. All Saints' would be completely responsible for pastoral visitation, lay workers, expenses, and the relief of the poor. The whole plan would require a team of ladies committed to visiting the section of the parish, before any mission services began, and money would be needed to put the proposed mission chapel into good order.

The plan sounds divisive but that was not Whitworth's intention. It was a mission which would not divide the chosen parish but save it from the necessity of sub-division. The Mission should not attempt to provide for all the spiritual needs of the parish nor should it duplicate the work of parish church. It seems strange with present day problems of retrenchment and amalgamation to think of sub-dividing parishes and building new churches, but such was the policy of the Victorian Church. If a parish was felt to be too large for whatever reasons, sometimes merely that its entire population could not be seated within the walls of the existing church, the parish should be divided and a new church built.

The district eventually selected was Pentonville, a parish of 4,000 people on the borders of Islington and Clerkenwell in north London. Work commenced after Easter 1888 in St Stephen's Mission Chapel which was situated in White Lion Street, 'a comparatively quiet and respectable street parallel to Pentonville Road'. The church had to pay a heavy rent for the mission house and chapel, and there was considerable expense in furnishing both. The former contained a room set apart for 'the exclusive use of lady workers where they can rest and have tea'. The Mission was formally opened on 28 April 1888 and, almost immediately, it was apparent that it would not function as originally intended. The people of the area had no concept of the Mission as a supplement to the work of their parish church, expecting it to provide a fuller provision of Sunday services and regular celebrations on Sunday mornings. The work proceeded at full speed and by May 1890, Whitworth reported that it was 'rapidly outgrowing our premises'. By the end of the year a second house in White Lion Street had been rented, partly to accommodate one of the curates on a full-time basis, and there were proposals to erect 'a plain iron building' in the garden for entertainment.

The Mission proved to be a constant drain on the resources of the parish and in June 1891, the resident curate at Pentonville was withdrawn, the clergy of the neighbouring churches of St Silas and St Mark providing pastoral oversight. The staff of All Saints' was reduced from six to five and the Mission itself was continued only through the generous donation of the sum of £300 p.a. by a Miss Olive Talbot. She died in October 1894 and, although another generous benefactor agreed to fund the mission until August 1895, the number of staff was again reduced by one and the work at Pentonville was scaled down accordingly. In 1895, Miss Talbot's sister, also a Miss Talbot, of Margam, offered £150 p.a. and a single donation of £300 to the Mission in memory of her sister, but obviously the situation could not continue indefinitely. Whatever the attendance had been like at the beginning, few people attended by July 1896. At that time Whitworth reported an average of 15 communicants every Sunday, 68 on Easter Day and 37 on Whitsunday. The Pentonville Mission was formally closed on 21 November 1897, Whitworth himself preaching at the closing service.

It is obviously difficult at this distance in time to make an accurate assessment of the Mission's work based upon the very scanty information available, but we cannot help but wonder if it was wise for All Saints' to undertake such a work. Apart from the drain of finance and energy, the enterprise bears all the marks of that rather patronising attitude to the poor, so much in evidence in late Victorian England. But, having said that, we do not doubt for a moment that it was motivated by the highest intention – to bring souls to Christ – and was staffed by the most well-meaning people. The Parish Paper of August 1892 gives us a clear picture of the kind of work done at the Mission. 'We were much pleased with the musical drill which we lately witnessed at the Mission House . . . and we congratulate Miss Cross and the other ladies for the success with which they have trained the girls. Physical training of this kind includes very valuable moral training, and we trust that girls who have thus learned to act together with unison and precision, will find their lessons to be fruitful in the discipline of life'.

William Whitworth's concern for the missionary activity of All Saints' had another and more unusual facet, that ran simultaneously with the work at Pentonville – the provision of church services in Welsh. It had come to his notice that many Welsh churchmen had complained that there was no church in west London at which they could hear a service in their own tongue. Furthermore, there were many Welsh-speaking small traders, particularly dairymen, in the immediate neighbourhood of the Church, together with 'many domestic servants and others who crave for ministrations in their native Welsh'.[11] Accordingly, he proposed that from 6 January 1889, a short Evensong and sermon would be held at 5.30 pm every Sunday for six weeks. Distinguished Welsh preachers would be invited to speak and, if the project was successful, a Welsh curate would be appointed, although money would be needed for a stipend! Evidently the initial response was sufficient to justify, in March 1890, the introduction of a quarterly choral celebration of the Eucharist, 'leaving the people to make their weekly communions in the churches most convenient'. But the enthusiasm did not last and the opening of a Welsh Church in Paddington (St David's, Paddington Green) in 1890 reduced the necessity of a Welsh ministry at All Saints', although 'it does not appear to have diminished the attendance at our own Welsh Evensong'. Whitworth also admitted at the same time that 'the crying necessity which suggested our effort two years ago no longer exists'. The work did continue, though numbers had diminished by November 1894 when the possibility of discontinuing this ministry was discussed. However, money was raised and the services lingered on until the end of the following year. The Welsh congregation, now 'very small', had decided in favour of their services conducted by a rota of clergy without a fixed pastor. Whitworth refused to co-operate, the Welsh curate was given notice on 30 September 1895 and the chaplaincy was formally terminated on 31 December of the same year.

Apart from these, his two favourite projects, Whitworth was confronted with the unchanging problems that have faced every Vicar of All Saints', Margaret Street: money and liturgy. For the first time in several years, the church had ended a year, 1887, without a deficit, there being a modest balance of £80 9s 0d, but the problems of operating an expensive church and choir on a very tight budget were never far away. In his review of the work of the church at the end of 1888 he delivered a rebuke to the wealthy congregation who were obviously parsimonious in their weekly giving. 'As a matter of fact, hundreds come to church in the most costly apparel of silk and fur, of gold and jewels, who apparently think a penny or threepence sufficient . . . And some give nothing at all . . . They thoughtlessly pass the bag as though it were an altogether exceptional duty to make an offering'.[12] The collection on Harvest Thanksgiving was minutely itemised: 2½ sovereigns, 12 crowns, 7 florins, 54 shillings, 72 sixpences, 59 threepences, 109 pence, 40 halfpennies, and one farthing. Total 356 coins: value £8 19s 6¼d. Time and time again Whitworth urged the congregation to be more generous in their giving. In March 1896 he reported that collections were 'very encouraging' though occasionally they were extremely low. On 26 January in that year – 'a fine day, with good congregations – one solitary half sovereign was the only offering of gold in the whole day'. In August 1904 'The offerings made in church have . . . been very small – sometimes, if viewed in comparison with the costly attire of the worshippers, we must say *painfully small*'.

The ritual at All Saints', though not as 'advanced' as it is today, was, in William Whitworth's day, still far enough advanced from the 'usual' late Victorian Anglican liturgy to be a source of concern. Whitworth was quite adamant that customs introduced by the Roman Catholic Church since 1549 could not be covered by the sanction of the Prayer Book, and that the services at All Saints' should in no way suggest any dissatisfactions with the prescribed formularies of the Church of England, 'or that the liberty accorded to her loyal children is insufficient for our aspirations'. He had almost no appreciation of music. 'I myself have no music in my soul, and the simplest services are to me the most spiritual', and the High Celebration on Sundays (the word Mass was never used) 'through my infirmity is not the source in which my soul finds utterance'. He reminded his people of those congregations 'whose churches are ceiled with cedar or painted with vermilion' and he urged them not to forget those parishes, as well as being thankful for their own church.

After the trial for ritual offences of Bishop Edward King of Lincoln in 1890, Whitworth moved swiftly to comply with the judgement of the Archbishop, and certain ceremonial changes were made in the liturgy from 6 January 1891. The mixing of water and wine in the chalice was to be made privately and apart; the manual acts of the celebrant during the celebration would henceforward be visible to all who

All Saints' Church, the east end, c. 1890

wished to see them; and the sign of cross would no longer be made at absolution or blessing. 'We should not clutch at the advantages of establishment while we repudiate the Archbishop's Court; or be thankful for the judgement as 'making for peace' while we still refuse to obey it'.[13]

On 13 September 1896, Pope Leo XIII issued his encyclical *Apostolicae Curae*, in which Anglican Orders were condemned as invalid through defect of both form and intention. Although the Archbishops of Canterbury and York issued a measured response *Saepius Officio* in the following year, Whitworth rushed to press almost immediately to defend the Church of England and to neutralise any effect the encyclical might have on his congregation. 'The decision of the Pope does not in the least affect Englishmen . . . It is now rather late in the day to refer to the Pope the question whether we are or are not a Church . . . or to suppose that we can be disturbed by any pronouncement of His Holiness upon our position. But the Bull is to be received with regret for the evidence it affords that Romanism is as far as ever from Catholicity'.[14] In the Parish Paper for November 1896 he attacked those Anglicans who were discontented and irritable with the Church of England, who would be more ready to spring to her defence if 'instead of accepting the Prayer Book as the authoritative utterance of the living church in England to be interpreted in the light of Catholic custom, we were to treat it as an inconvenient rule, to be followed only as far as the law compels, to be explained away when possible; to be superseded by Missal, or Breviary of Sarum, or of Rome'. '. . . We have adhered to Mr Upton Richards' great principle of accepting the Prayer Book as our standard, interpreting it in the light of Catholic precedent, and in the most Catholic sense that it will fairly bear, but never setting it aside'. He never accepted the Roman doctrine of transubstantiation' and 'we do not suppose that . . . our worship is made more accept-able by the Sacrament being reserved in a tabernacle on the altar'. By 1901 he was being urged to introduce radical change by turning Morning Prayer into a service without music of any description, thereby so minimizing its significance that the congregation would be induced to attend the following 'Choral Celebration'. Whitworth's reply was that the people of God were called to the Divine Office as much as the Divine Service and during Lent 1902 he urged the congregation regularly to attend the daily offices. Incense was, of course, not used, because there was no reference to it in the Prayer Book of 1549 and, therefore, Whitworth deemed it to be among the 'multitude' of ceremonial which the Preface to that Prayer Book declared to be 'put away'.

William Whitworth appears to have been a powerful preacher, and his obituary in the *Church Times* spoke of 'the keen analytical mind gradually unfolding the chosen subject, spread it out in detail, developed it so as to touch modern life, and closed by a brief but powerful exhortation'. Probably his most productive, if not remarkable sermon, was that preached in the Chapel of St John's College, Cambridge, on Sexagesima Sunday, 28 January 1883. He took for his text Hosea 4:6, 'My people are destroyed for lack of knowledge'. His theme was that the working classes had turned against religion in general because they knew so little about it. He pointed out that ignorance could not be met by ignorance, and that the working classes would never be won by ill-instructed teachers, and was it possible that St John's College might be able to do something by adopting some poor parish in London. A number of undergraduates were fired by enthusiasm by the sermon, and its subsequent publication served to keep the fire going. The idea was discussed at various meetings and eventually the Lady Margaret Mission in Walworth, and others elsewhere in South London, were founded.

Looking back at the ministry of William Allen Whitworth, we wonder whether he was ever really at ease with the parish. He was an impetuous man by nature and succeeded in upsetting a good proportion of the congregation within weeks of his arrival. The somewhat conservative and traditional atmosphere cannot have been altogether to the liking of the vigorous 46-year-old church 'builder' from Hammersmith. His ministry at St John's was marked by expansion and innovation, but at All Saints' expansion was impossible and innovation was undesirable and suspect, and this greatly restricted his natural talent and ability. Neither of his two innovations, Welsh services and the Pentonville Mission, lasted more than a few years. Unlike his two predecessors, he chose to live in the Vicarage, against the advice of the Churchwardens, thereby breaking with precedent and establishing a new arrangement. He always admitted that he had no ear for music and could not appreciate the full beauty of the liturgy. Within a few months of his arrival, he had replaced all Berdmore Compton's curates with his own from Hammersmith, possibly intending some great transformation based on his work there. Without further details it would be impossible to do more than guess.

In a sermon of 1904, his vigorous analytical mind was shown to have led him fearlessly through the fray of intellectual debate on aspects of contemporary theology. '. . . Yet we are not disquieted. We welcome the assistance of scholarship, criticism, and commonsense, yet we continue in the faith, grounded and settled, and are not moved away from the hope of the Gospel which we have received'.

Whitworth presided over the parish at a time of

great change, not least its rapid depopulation. The population had fallen to nearly 2,000 in 1902, a figure which included a large number of Jews. He firmly resisted any liturgical advancement, taking his stand on the rubrics of the Prayer Book, but at a time when other Anglo-Catholic churches were adopting full Roman practices. He was clearly a man of great talent and we incline to the view that this never found its fullest expression at All Saints', and the resulting frustration contributed to his comparatively early death. He was not in the best of health for the last few years of his incumbency, and was seriously ill in the autumn of 1902, to the point where he was not expected to live. He died, one week after an operation for cancer of the bowel, in the early hours of Sunday 12 March 1905. His last article, in a special Lenten letter, bewailed the declining size of congregations on Sunday evenings.

His body was taken to the Sisters' Mortuary Chapel where the first Office of the Dead was sung. On Wednesday evening, it was brought back to the Church where it was received by the clergy and taken into the Chancel. The 'Office of Remembrance of the Faithful Departed' was sung, and at its conclusion a watch was kept by the Sisters and others throughout the night. On the following morning Holy Communion was celebrated by the Bishop of London at 8.00 am, and the Bishop of Kensington presided at the High Celebration at 10.00 am. The body was subsequently taken to Brookwood Cemetery and interred in the plot of land belonging to the parish of St Alban, Holborn. The committal was performed by Willoughby Carter, Vicar of St Matthias, Earl's Court, a former curate of All Saints', and during the interment, a memorial service was held at All Saints', conducted by Canon the Marquess of Normanby, a long standing friend of Whitworth.

Since his four sons were still at school or

VICAR, J.H.POGH 195~
C.H.GOULING-BIRD.
W.CARTER, H.J.T.BENNETTS

William Allen Whitworth (standing on the far left), with his curates, 1900

university, the PCC felt that an appropriate memorial would be a fund to enable them to complete their education. Mrs Louisa Whitworth was subsequently presented with cheques totalling £1121. William and Louisa Whitworth had four sons: William Hervey Allen Whitworth (1887–1960), Headmaster of Framlingham 1929–1940; George Elwes Allen Whitworth (1888–1969), Vicar of Great St Mary's, Cambridge 1947–1954; Edward Eric Allen

Whitworth (1889–1971), Headmaster of Tonbridge and then Bradfield College; and Cyril Clinton Allen Whitworth (1890–1955), a priest of the Society of St John the Evangelist.

Louisa Whitworth was a resilient and formidable lady who enjoyed travelling and spent a good deal of time in Italy and Switzerland. After her husband's death, she moved with her children to the family holiday home at Bexhill. She later returned to London to live near Baker Street. In 1920–25, her son George was Vicar of St Andrew's, Bethnal Green, and served a year as Mayor of Bethnal Green. Being unmarried at the time he invited his mother to serve as Mayoress, a role which brought her much pleasure. She later went to live with her son Eric while he was Headmaster of Tonbridge School and from there moved to Oxford to live, appropriately, with the All Saints' Sisters at St John's Home. She died there in 1952 at the age of ninety-nine.

CHAPTER FOUR

THE TEACHER
GEORGE HOLDEN
1905–1908

'I have always been brought up to say
quite frankly what I believe to be the truth,
and I am afraid that it is too late
for me to alter, even if were desirable
to do so'
(George Frederick Holden, writing in the Parish
Paper for March 1906.)

No picture appears to have survived of George Holden, 4th Vicar, 1905–1908. This pyx, with its cover, was given to him by the people of St John's, Wilton Road, and was bequeathed on his death, to the All Saints' Sisters

GEORGE FREDERICK HOLDEN

Born: 26 February 1858
Pembroke College, Oxford 1879–1881
Deacon 1881   Priest 1882
Curate of St Saviour's, Everton 1881–1884
Curate of St Peter's, Eaton Square 1884–1905
(Curate in Charge of St John's, Wilton Road
1888–1905)
Vicar of All Saints', Margaret Street 1905–1908
Died: 3 March 1908

AFTER the death of Whitworth, the benefice of All Saints' was vacant for about three months before being offered to and accepted by George Frederick Holden, Curate-in-Charge of the Church of St John the Evangelist, Wilton Road. Holden, a forty-seven year old widower, is the least remembered Vicar of All Saints. Instituted on 1 June 1905, his tenure lasted only a little more than two and a half years before he died from influenza in March 1908. Reading through accounts of his powerful and successful incumbency at Wilton Road, his brief ministry at All Saints', and the glowing tributes paid to him after his death, we see him as a priest of considerable talent and spirituality who, had he survived, might well have been numbered among the greatest incumbents of the church. As it is, his tragically early death at the age of only fifty cut short a life of great promise at All Saints', and we can only record his brief ministry there with profound sadness.

We have been unable to discover much of his early life. He was born in Everton, Lancashire, in 1858 into an evangelical family the son of Thomas Patrick Holden, a master cabinet maker and Mary née Fitzpatrick and went to Pembroke College, Oxford in the late 1870s. His obituary in the *Church Times* mentions 'an early business training in Liverpool', which helped in later years to give his appeal 'special attraction for men of a robust type'.[1] He was ordained deacon in 1881 and priest in the following year, serving his title at the Church of St Saviour, Everton, a benefice in the gift of evangelical trustees. Evidently he wished to move to London because, in the spring of 1884, he applied for a vacant minor canonry at St Paul's Cathedral. He was unsuccessful, but during the course of that visit met John Storrs, the Vicar of St Peter's, Eaton Square. Storrs was impressed with Holden's abilities and invited him to join his staff with effect from August.

He was appointed as assistant to the Reverend J. W. C. Burnaby, Priest-in-Charge of the daughter church of St John the Evangelist, Wilton Road, and it was here that the greater part of his earthly ministry was spent.

St John's, Wilton Road was built during the incumbency of George Howard Wilkinson, who left St Peter's in 1883 to become Bishop of Truro. He had a flourishing ministry and it was decided that, since the church was full every Sunday, more churches were needed. Accordingly, St John's was built in 1874 and a lease was taken on St Peter's Chapel, Palace Street. The district of the parish in which St John's was built was one of extreme poverty comprising a warren of little streets where vice was rife. It was said that patrons leaving the Victoria Palace Theatre any evening could buy children for prostitution. The site of the church was originally part of the Grosvenor Basin, an unloading place for barges, and the composition of the ground was such that the church had to be built on piles. The foundation stone was laid on St Peter's Eve 1873 and the nave was ready for use by February 1874. The completed church, designed by Sir Arthur Blomfield, was consecrated on 4 July of that year.

On the departure of Burnaby in 1888, George Holden was appointed to succeed him as Priest-in-Charge of St John's, and there he remained for the next seventeen years. The basis of Holden's ministry at St John's was his vision of the necessity of educating believers into the essentials of the Christian faith, and he built up a devout congregation 'who should have a vital knowledge of those great truths of History and of Revelation upon which the Catholic Faith depends'. He realised, as all the great saints in every age have realised, 'that it is upon a living knowledge of the Bible itself that the most steadfast spiritual experience rests'. His evangelical origins had given him a thorough grounding in scripture and this he put to good effect by establishing a series of Bible lectures given at midday on Wednesdays to a congregation of 'leisured' people who gathered from all parts of London, and again on Wednesday evenings, in a slightly simpler form, to an equally large congregation of those who had been at work all day. Many years later, members of those congregations testified to the 'amazing freshness' of those lectures. Holden was careful to explain all ambiguous or difficult words, but was never pedantic on points of grammar or textual criticism, nor did he attempt to convey the finer and more obscure points of biblical theology. 'His chief emphasis lay on the broad principles of truth, the great doctrines of the Catholic Faith, and the practical lessons of duty that lay hid in the sacred Word'.[2]

From the study of the Bible, he passed on to the study of doctrine. He lectured on the 39 Articles, dealing exhaustively with all the fundamental doctrines of the Church and, suprisingly, spreading the course over a period of three years. From doctrine, he moved on to the study of history, where he displayed an intimate and accurate knowledge not only of church history but the general history of the European nations. 'He saw it clearly and wholly with a wide and accurate vision, which preserved him from those errors of despair, disproportion and prejudice, that are so fatal to the less careful student'.[3]

One of his attentive hearers testified to the fact that audiences 'were never left merely with the sense that we had acquired information and learned dates. We felt that we were living in a new fellowship, and that the world . . . was a wider and richer one than we had dreamed'.[4]

There were monthly Addresses to Communicants in which he laid stress on the frequency of Communion and of sound preparation beforehand.

From these beginnings he developed an increasingly significant ministry to the penitent. His preaching appears to have been of a very high order and attracted an eclectic congregation from all over London. '. . . His sermons carried us away with their ring of triumphant conviction, and sent us back to our work, happy, hopeful, humble and reassured. He gave us . . . not scraps of disordered learning, but great principles of action, illuminating insight into the ways of God in human life, conviction of the coherence and reasonableness of the Catholic Faith, and steadied us for blithe and resolute service in the duties of the day'.[5] This comprehensive ministry was effected against the background of a church with few external signs of the Catholic tradition. Mattins remained the main Sunday service until 1896, and eucharistic vestments were not introduced until after his death in 1908, but such externals were of little concern to Holden, who was not a ritualist. He followed the great Tractarians in regarding holiness as far more important than the ritual. It is a clear tribute to George Holden's powers of judgement that he was prepared to defer the introduction of the Eucharist as the central act of worship until, after ten years of patient and consistent teaching of eucharistic doctrine, he judged both the time right to make this change and that there would be no misgivings on the part of the congregation.

In August 1898, George Holden married a Miss Florence Walker at St Peter's, Eaton Square, and for six years they led a happy married life at St John's. She died in 1904, a blow from which her grieving husband was slow to recover. His first and quite natural instinct was to remain where he was and to continue his work with renewed vigour, but Arthur Winnington-Ingram (Bishop of London, 1901–1939) persuaded him to leave and to accept the living of All Saints'. It proved to be a wise decision. His wife's illness and death had put Holden under great strain and stress, and the sadness and pain of parting from his beloved congregation after more than twenty years only made matters worse in the short term. But he soon threw himself whole-heartedly into his new sphere of work where his natural ability found new fields for expression.

His appointment was announced in April 1905 and in the Parish paper for May he wrote 'I undertake this charge with fear and trembling . . . The last two years, as some of you may know, have been to me years of very exceptional strain and stress, and therefore I am afraid that it will not be possible for me to take up my full duties at once'. Holden proposed to preach every Sunday, morning and evening, in June and then take a prolonged rest for three months 'in obedience to the urgent representations of my doctor', coming into residence in the parish in October. The induction took place on 1 June, Ascension Day, at 5 pm and, walking immediately in front of the new vicar, was the venerable figure of Prebendary Berdmore Compton, his mind no doubt casting back to his own induction in the same church more than thirty years earlier. In his sermon, the Bishop reminded the congregation that he expected his parish priests to be prophets, evangelists, pastors and teachers. 'His sermons are not to be mere appeals to the emotions but he has to teach line upon line, here a little, there a little, the whole Catholic Faith, committed to his trust'.[6]

Holden soon proved to be a vigorous and active vicar with a clear insight into the strengths and weaknesses of the church. He began his incumbency by praising the staff of clergy, inherited from William Whitworth, as hard-working to such an extent that they found themselves unable to take their day off during the week. This had to be rectified, since no body of individuals could possibly go on without adequate rest and recreation. 'There is a popular regard, widespread in the lay mind, that the clergy work one day in the week, and play on the other six'.[7] St John's, Wilton Road had enjoyed a very high standard of music and Holden found the musical traditions of All Saints' quite up to his old standards. His only criticism in this regard was that the morning service was a little too long, especially on great festivals, but he showed great care not to antagonize the formidable figure of William Stevenson Hoyte who had been appointed organist of All Saints' by William Upton Richards as far back as 1868. 'You may be sure that I shall not do anything in a hurry, and I have far too hearty an appreciation of Dr ·Hoyte's thirty-seven years' service . . . to do anything without his cordial co-operation'.[8] He gave a broad hint that he expected to do something about cleaning the church, some of the beauties of which have been obscured by 'the dust and dirt of dusty and dirty London'.

Although St John's had developed an eclectic congregation under Holden's ministry, he was genuinely surprised by the great distances travelled, even in 1905, by members of the congregation to reach All Saints' Church. 'I am a little puzzled at present to know how I am to find time and opportunity for visiting . . .'.[9] He placed great store by the social and sociable relations that he had had with the congregation at St John's, and introduced the custom of holding a conversazione at intervals. The first was held on 8 November between 8 and 11 pm and was a great success, more than 300 people attending. He also made known his intention to be 'at home' each Monday from 9.15 to 10.30 pm for any of the congregation who wished to call. There is an interesting reference to smoking in his article for January 1905 which suggests that smoking was still a habit that was socially frowned upon in spite of being widespread. One of Holden's former colleagues at St. John's, the Reverend G. G. Richards, subsequently Vicar of Upper Teddington, had achieved unexpected notoriety in the press by inviting the men of his congregation back to his vicarage for 'a quiet pipe'. Holden, although he hesitated to issue the invitation in such a detailed form, did announce that it would be unwise to ignore 'the social power of tobacco, which is deservedly very great'.

In February 1906 he referred to his early comment about the liturgy being too long and added that this was partly due to the increasing number of communicants at the High Celebration on Sunday (the word 'Mass' was still unthinkable). A non-communicating celebration was still the normal pattern at that time, and Holden urged his congregation to receive the Sacrament at an earlier celebration. 'The early morning is undoubtedly the time for reception, and it is my strong belief that those who have ever given it a fair trial find the spiritual benefit so great that Sunday is not quite the same to then when . . . they have missed that wonderful meeting with Our Lord in the sweet morning hour'. The only communicants that he expected to see at the High Celebration were either the elderly or the physically infirm, and the sight of so many young people communicating at that service caused him much distress. At the same time he warned that attendance at Mattins could never take the place of attendance at the Holy Eucharist. Evidently his strictures against communion at the High Celebration were not at all well received in certain quarters since he reported in March 1906 the receipt of some letters of complaint. Holden was quite unmoved. 'I have always been brought up to say quite frankly what I believe to be the truth, and I am afraid that it is too late for me to alter, even if it were desirable to do so'.

It may be unfair to William Whitworth to say that

All Saints' had receded from the fullest expression of the Catholic tradition within the Church of England, but it is true to say that George Holden was much more advanced in this regard than his predecessor. In 1906 he re-established a ward of the Confraternity of the Blessed Sacrament, and in the same year All Saints' was affiliated to the English Church Union under the name 'Margaret Street and Mayfair Branch'. This latter decision was prompted by the genuine concern both of Holden, and indeed throughout the Church of England, at government proposals to transfer control of church schools to the State. 'I confess that it has quickened a resolution which for some time has been forming in my mind as to whether we of All Saints' ought not to have a branch of our own . . I am quite certain not merely on the Education question but on other questions also there is more need than ever for the English Church Union.'.[10]

Holden was well aware of the beauty of the building that he had inherited and of the Church's reputation for a well-presented liturgy, and he made several (successful) appeals in the Parish Paper for donations to be applied to meet specific needs. In June 1906 he appealed for funds to purchase two frontals, one red and one violet; a set of white silk vestments; two copes, one red and one black; three stoles, one green, one violet and one white; twelve white silk alms bags with oak handles; a pair of silver cruets; and fourteen boys' surplices; at a total cost of £159. All of them were acquired within a year. It would be impossible to identify which of these items still survive in All Saints' today, though we may reasonably assume that the white silk alms bags and the boys' surplices have long since departed, but his most important addition to the appearance of All Saints' was seven sanctuary lamps hanging before the altar, of which six are still in use. The lamps were given by various donors, most of whom wished to remain anonymous. They cost £50 each and were reproductions of the silver lamps hanging in the Church of the Holy Sepulchre in Jerusalem and copied from the set in St Alban's, Teddington.

Holden was not a man to suffer fools gladly and was capable of using a direct and acerbic wit to great effect on such occasions as he found to be appropriate. On one particular occasion, when an anonymous individual sent him a number of large books, all arguing against vaccination and in favour of the use of herbs in the cure of diseases, he replied publicly by way of the Parish Paper: 'I can assure my anonymous friend that I have no time to read them, and that, if I had time, I have other things to study, and the great volumes only cumber the ground in my study. I should be grateful if the affliction might cease, otherwise I shall be compelled to turn the books into spills for my Monday Evening Tobacco Parliament. I am absolutely convinced that vaccination is one of the greatest boons ever bestowed on the human race, and when I can find the necessary time, I shall use it, not in reading anti-vaccination literature, but in going to one of my numerous medical friends in the congregation and getting vaccinated'.[11]

He published very little, and only two of his works are of any size: *The Holy Ghost the Comforter,* published in 1908, and *The Special Bases of the Anglican Claim,* published in 1903. A second and revised edition of the latter was published in 1916 with notes by F. C. N. Hicks and S. L. Ollard. It is a pity that his productivity was so low since the little he did publish shows a clarity and incisiveness of thought. His real skill lay in oratory, and his lengthy lectures, begun at St John's and continued at All Saints', were popular and well-attended. *The Special Bases of the Anglican Claim* was based on a series of lectures delivered at St John's in Lent 1903. In

78

response to the requests of his friends and congregation he agreed to prepare them for publication; his object was to describe some of the most distinctive characteristics of the Church of England, and the five lectures were headed 'The Appeal to Antiquity', 'Comprehensiveness', 'Continuity'; Reasonableness' and 'Nationality'.

'The Appeal to Antiquity' emphasized one of the first great principles of the Oxford Movement – that the Church of England was not a schismatic body, riddled with heresy, but, in the words of John Keble, 'The Apostolical Church of this Realm'. The English Reformers of the sixteenth century had maintained the claim that they were going back to the early days, searching scriptures and writings of ancient authors to see how far the Christianity of their own generation had fallen away from the faith of the Saints. Holden quoted, as proof of the great chasm between the Roman and Anglican Churches, the tendency of the Roman Church to erect 'matters of pious opinion into dogmas', such as the prerogatives of the papacy, the position of the Virgin Mary in the scheme of salvation and the invocation of the Saints. He quotes Cardinal Manning from *The Temporal Mission of the Holy Ghost*: 'The appeal to antiquity is both a treason and a heresy . . . the Church has no antiquity. It rests upon its own supernatural and perpetual consciousness . . . The only divine evidence to us of what was primitive is the witness and the voice of the Church at this hour'. This was anathema to Holden. 'The Church of England acknowledged that Churches may err, and therefore in the light of that fact she goes back to primitive times for information. I believe that God blesses such humility, and that the ecclesiastical pride which is afraid to admit the possibility of error or mistake, in the long run must encounter the divine resistance'.

In his lecture on 'Comprehensiveness', he

recognized that the divisions of the Church of England were a potent weapon in the hands of any Roman Catholic. 'They are deep enough and wide enough, let us sorrowfully admit; but they are not so deep and not so wide as our adversaries would make out', and in any case Christianity of whatever denomination would be unwise to press the mark of absolute unity and uniformity as a credential of the true Church to the exclusion of all other marks. If the Church was to be defined as 'One, Holy, Catholic and Apostolic', then it should be as much 'Holy' as 'One'. The holiness of the Church and its members was as important as the unity of the Church. But neither should be pressed as the absolute credential of a true Church. Holden quoted the Donatist schism of the 4th century, their concept of the Church being that of an exclusive club of the good and the approved. 'If it be asked which mark Our Lord would select should a collision occur between the interests of unity and holiness, if I read my gospels aright I have no hesitation in saying, that such is His intense love for each soul that he would subordinate unity to holiness'. Holden argued the case, if not for disunity, then certainly for diversity in a very competent way. The love of God for the individual soul and the development of the individual character; the im-perfect accounts of Scripture; the diverse qualities of the apostles; the withering away of the great heresies of the early centuries; and the careful, diplomatic construction of the Creed. 'With a shrewdness and a nicety like that of some ablest and most sustained course of statecraft and a cabinet policy, it went on adhering to the complex original idea, and balancing one tendency in it by another'. To Holden's mind, the inclusiveness of the Church of England was one of its glories and, as such, it bore strong resemblance to the primitive Church. 'It is perfectly easy but disastrous in the extreme for either

80

side to call the other traitors, and to demand that the Church of England shall be exclusively moulded after its fashion . . . Let each school learn to tolerate and to see the good points in other schools, and engage in a generous rivalry as to which shall do the most for that Master's cause which is dear to all'.

In his lecture on 'Continuity', he stressed the role of the Church of England as the modern representative of the ancient Ecclesia Anglicana, and that the Church of England was the only real claimant in this field. Continuity of language, boundary, law, custom, institution and literature, all served to identify the Church of England as the true Catholic Church in England. The one exception to which Holden gave only scant attention was the casting aside of the jurisdiction of the papacy, but he used the excuse that the English Church before the Henrician Reformation was always restive under papal exactions, and that the Reformation was only the culmination of a long struggle beginning with the Constitutions of Clarendon of 1164. 'It was a resolute national determination, headed by the king, to throw off the foreign yoke, which had become a burden beyond bearing. There was not the slightest idea of setting up a new church, or of creating a new kind of ministry, or a fresh spiritual discipline imported from Geneva'. This statement is arguably true, but Holden appears not to have considered the Genevan influences on Archbishop Cranmer in compiling the Prayer Book of 1552 which, with minor changes, is the same as the 1662 Book in use in Holden's day.

His fourth lecture dealt with what he described as 'the sweet reasonableness of the Church of England' in five different ways. Firstly, the Church had a very healthy attitude towards the miraculous. Holden held that it was essential to believe in the gospel miracles, and in the great central miracle of the Resurrection. But the Church had a duty not to pander to credulity

81

or to prejudice the whole case for the gospel miracles by supporting and believing in such 'childish examples of the supernatural, such as the flight of the Virgin's House to Loretto, the liquefaction of the blood of St Januarius, and the crop of more or less doubtful marvels at Lourdes'. Whether Holden was right or wrong in describing such occurrences as childish and impossible is, to some extent, a matter for the individual to determine, since belief in such happenings is not an essential of the Faith. But there is much in his language at this stage which indicates a resurgence of his early evangelical upbringing – a kind of commonsense, 'no nonsense' approach, which could lead to a denial of the activity of divine grace in such happenings. Holden was certain that one of the great strengths of the Church of England was its reserve in the matter of defining truth. He referred to it as a kind of Christian agnosticism which, by virtue of its unwillingness to over-define, was able to sympathize with those who felt themselves unable to define fully their beliefs. 'We do not want the Church of Christ to be looked upon as a kind of oracle, always professing to give a full and final answer to every question . . . It seems to me that a reasonable position like this is much more likely to commend itself to, and to win, the agnostic unbeliever than any amount of loud claims to know everything'. He supported a critical examination of the texts of Holy Scripture and praised the authors of *Lux Mundi*, published in 1889, as 'a body of men who have spoken with unique power to the educated Christians of the day who are beset on all sides by onslaughts upon the Catholic Faith'.

Holden had great sympathy and compassion for the doubter and urged his readers to react similarly to those plagued by intellectual doubts about some aspects of the Christian faith, and quoted the case of Charles Bradlaugh (1833–1891), the free-thinking

MP for Northampton, as an example of one with a devout but bright and enquiring mind who had lost his faith because of insensitive handling by his parish priest.

His fifth and last lecture, entitled 'Nationality', is the least attractive and the most dated of all but, since it formed part of his argument for the ideal distinctive claims of Anglicanism, it should be mentioned. Anglicanism was intimately bound up with Englishness, and the two fused to form a good moral code for the guidance of every Christian. A few sentences will suffice. 'To England . . . more than to any other nation the downtrodden and oppressed have turned . . . for sympathy and help. When Spain threw off the French yoke, when Greece effected her national independence, when Italy emerged a free and united nation, it must be confessed they owed much to English sympathy, to English blood, and to English gold . . . In philanthropic enterprise, unbounded by race or class, England easily stands pre-eminent . . . To this may we not add that in kindness to animals the English people stand far ahead of any other nation . . . English straightforwardness . . . largely accounts for the permanency of our rule in India . . . If the union between nationality and religion . . . has resulted in such a type of character, we may well think that God has blessed the mark of nationality'. Enough said!

Such passages in his writings have indeed dated badly, but were Holden alive today, he would probably be the first to admit the fact and to revise them in the light of contemporary theology. George Holden was a gifted orator and communicator as attendances at his Wednesday lunchtime lectures bear witness, and he would no doubt have recognized the transience of many of his images and illustrations, and been able to convey the great truths of Christianity equally well to a different generation in a different way.

Looking back at what little we know of his life and work, eighty years after his death, we feel a certain sadness that this extremely talented priest should have died, from influenza and pneumonia, at the tragically early age of fifty. There were many interesting facets to the man of which now we have only the briefest glimpse. There are fleeting references in his writings to a clear fascination with the whole phenomenon of Eastern Orthodoxy in general and with the Russian Orthodox Church in particular, and this may account for his strident anti-Romanism at times. He regarded the Oxford Movement as a way of injecting some kind of life into the dull and dreary 18th century Church of England and, at the same time, of preventing secession to the Church of Rome. He was highly critical of the anti-ritualists in the Church because, by attempting to suppress the outward signs of Catholicism in the Church of England, they were playing directly into the hands of the Romans. 'It is the Catholic claim of the Church of England which in this country the Church of Rome hates and dreads. The clear definite duty of all try-hearted Anglicans is . . . to assert their claim to the title 'Catholic', and to all that the title implies in the possession of life-giving sacraments and sacerdotal powers'.

George Frederick Holden died on 3 March 1908, after a brief but acute illness, to the great grief of the congregations of St John's, Wilton Road and All Saints', Margaret Street. In a long obituary, the *Church Times* mourned the passing of 'a most remarkable teacher of the Catholic Faith . . . It is impossible to estimate the loss [he] will be to All Saints', but only those who knew him best can realize what an enormous loss he will be to hundreds all over the country, who looked to him as their spiritual guide. What he had done in three years at All Saints' can never be estimated at its true value; his wonderful tact, never failing love, and deep spiritual power made an impression that will never be effaced'. During his last illness he was visited by the Bishops of Kensington and London, the latter calling twice on the evening of his death. Bishop Winnington-Ingram had a high regard for George Holden and was much distressed by his death. In July 1924 he attended a reunion of past and present members of the congregation and friends of St John's, Wilton Road, to celebrate the 50th anniversary of the consecration of the Church, and spoke warmly of his memories of Holden. 'I believe we owe a great deal to that man . . . and I shall never forget, when I did drag him away from St John's to All Saints', Margaret Street, being with that saint as he died'.

His body rested temporarily in the mortuary chapel of the All Saints' Sisters across the street from the church until after Evensong on the following Sunday, when it was brought back to All Saints' where Vespers of the Dead was sung in the presence of the Bishop of Kensington. A watch was kept all night by the Sisters and members of the congregation. On Monday morning, Morning Prayer was said at 5.30 am and the Eucharist offered at 6.00, 6.30 and 7.30 am, and a Solemn Requiem at 9.30 am in the presence of the Bishop of London. After the service, his body was taken to Market Bosworth in Stafford-shire where he was laid to rest beside his wife, only a few miles away from the resting place of Berdmore Compton at Atherstone.

Henry Mackay, 5th Vicar, 1908–1934

CHAPTER FIVE

THE PREACHER
HENRY MACKAY
1908–1934

'He was one of the, perhaps few, great preachers of his day. Of his sermons he wrote, and read, every word, without giving much impression of reading. They were invariably as fresh, topical, and up-to-date, as they were devoid of clichés, platitudes, a word too many, a word too few. Always they were penetrating, packed with knowledge of contemporary and pristine human nature, flashing of phrase, impossible to ignore, difficult to forget'

(H. A. Wilson, *Received with Thanks*, London, 1940, p. 150.)

HENRY FALCONAR BARCLAY MACKAY

Born: 22 March 1864
Merton College, Oxford 1884–1887
Cuddesdon Theological College 1887–1888
Deacon 1888   Priest 1889
Curate of All Saints', Margaret Street, 1888–1891
Curate of All Saints', Clifton 1891–1895
Sub-Librarian of Pusey House, Oxford 1895–1896
Librarian of Pusey House, Oxford 1896–1908
Vicar of All Saints', Margaret Street 1908–1934
Prebendary of Brownswood, St Paul's Cathedral
1920–1934
Canon Residentiary of Gloucester Cathedral 1934–35
Died: 20 April 1936

IN CONTRAST to the three previous interregna of 1873, 1886 and 1905, each of which had lasted for several months, that of 1908 lasted only a few days. George Holden died on 3 March, and on 30 March his successor addressed a letter to his new flock, expressing his pleasure at the prospect of returning to the church in which he had once served as a curate. Bishop Winnington-Ingram's choice had fallen on Henry Falconar Barclay Mackay, the forty-four year old Librarian of Pusey House, Oxford. Mackay is a unique figure among the twelve Vicars of the church in that he was the only one to have served on the staff as a curate. After leaving Cuddesdon Theological College in 1888, he served his title at All Saints' under William Whitworth, leaving in 1891 to go to Bristol because he could not agree with Whitworth's acceptance of all the clauses of the Lincoln Judgement.

Henry Mackay was born at Milford Haven in 1864 at Priory Lodge, the home of his grandmother. He was the eldest of the five children of Captain Alexander Mackay, RN and his wife, Alice Starbuck. His mother came from an old Quaker family, and throughout his life Mackay retained something of the puritanical and contemplative character of that sect. He read theology at Merton College, Oxford, where he took a first, and after a year at Cuddesdon he was ordained to a title at All Saints', Margaret Street, spending most of his time working at Pentonville Mission. In 1891 he moved to All Saints', Clifton, in Bristol, until he was asked by Robert Ottley (1856–1933), the Principal of Pusey House, Oxford, to go there as Librarian. He stayed in Oxford for twelve years until his return to All Saints' in 1908. It was at Oxford that his considerable talent for preaching came to the fore. Mackay was rather shy and stiff in manner, and this reserve, unfortunately, never left him for the remainder of his life. He could be alarmingly offhand, or so it seemed, to new undergraduates, but those who took the trouble to get to know him found that the initial impression of aloofness soon wore off. 'Unreserved he certainly was not; but behind his reserve was a brilliant humour, a fund of goodness, and a very human heart . . . here was no mere High Church curate, but a very attractive and accomplished companion, who could become a most delightful friend'.[1] He acquired a reputation as a preacher of unusual power and clarity, and his influence in his latter years was considerable. Though he was innately shy, his somewhat austere and clipped manner has been ascribed partly to his strong devotion to Cardinal Henry Manning. Before going up to Merton in 1884, Mackay spent several happy years as a pupil of the Reverend Rowley Lascelles, Rector of Lavington in Sussex. Cardinal Manning had been Rector of Lavington in the 1830s and memories of his ministry still survived forty years later during Mackay's stay there. It sometimes seemed as if something of Manning's severity had overcome the basic human kindness in Mackay. But it was only a superficial severity, and it masked a very real gentleness and goodness of heart, which contributed so much to his success at Oxford in attracting and influencing some of the best undergraduates of his time there. Many of them found their way to All Saints' as his curates. On his return to All Saints' in 1908 he brought with him the reputation for original and intellectual preaching and he quickly attracted a congregation which filled the church until his departure in 1934.

Although he was inducted as far back as 1908, we now pass, incredibly, into the sphere of living memory, as there are several members of the present congregation who remember him in his last years, and one of his curates is still alive at the time of writing. Mackay's death in 1936 was recorded by a massive obituary in the *Church Times* that occupied most of a page, and in April 1937 a memoir consisting of collected reminiscences was published by Sidney Dark. A large number of his sermons and addresses were collected and published in twelve volumes, the last posthumously in 1937, and a further brief memoir (with others) by H. A. Wilson, appeared in 1940. So there is a great fund of material, documentary and otherwise, from which we can reconstruct a good deal of the public life, thought and spirituality of Henry Mackay. We find ourselves in a position to speak with much more clarity and authority about the life of the fifth Vicar than was possible with the somewhat shadowy figures of the first four. The word 'life' should not be taken to include 'private' or 'family' life. Mackay was essentially a reticent man and would have considered talking about himself as extra-ordinarily bad-mannered. He rarely made even the smallest reference to his private life and he showed no great desire for human friendship and, therefore, he was a very difficult person to get to know. But in the pulpit Mackay was at his brilliant best and for twenty-five years there flowed a stream of inspired and inspiring sermons from All Saints' Church. Some have dated, many now sound slightly old-fashioned, but in all of them it is possible to discern a high degree of visionary ability in interpreting the scriptures, and much of his work retains a certain amount of vividness and immediacy.

Mackay began his work at All Saints' by telling the parish that his initial intention was to carry on the work of George Holden 'by his methods and in his spirit', and he refused to predict what changes he might make or how the parish might develop. He did make the point that the work of All Saints' was of such a high intensity that the clergy team should be brought up to full strength as soon as possible to avoid any unnecessary nervous and mental strain, and he reminded the congregation that his two immediate predecessors had died in office, maybe with the implication that he himself did not intend to go the same way.

The induction was held on Ascension Day, Thursday 28 May, at 5 pm. It may seem a rather odd time, but it was chosen to avoid clashing with any of the full round of services on Ascension Day. The Eucharist was celebrated at 6.00, 7.00 and 8.00 am. Matins was said at 10.30 am, followed by a High Celebration at 11.00 am, at which the Bishop of Bloemfontein was preacher. The day was rounded off by Evensong, Procession and Sermon at 8.30 pm. The Church was filled to capacity for the induction, and over sixty clergy from all parts of the Diocese of London joined in the long procession up the centre aisle to the sanctuary. The Bishop, vested in cope and mitre, took his seat below the altar steps, and the office proceeded 'with a dignity and beauty that is seldom equalled in our churches'. He preached on the text 'Behold I see heaven opened, and the Son of Man standing at the right hand of God' (Acts 7:56). He urged Mackay always to have with him this vision of the ascended Christ as an inspiration for his work, 'and when that work on earth is over, may you, with the same perfect submission as St Stephen, and as your immediate predecessor had, lay down your life with the humble prayer, "Lord Jesus, receive my spirit".'

One of Mackay's first tasks was the provision of another altar for the church. Several people had told him that a side altar was a priority requirement because the celebrant was so far away from the congregation at weekday services. Mackay reiterated this point, remarking that 'the clergy make efforts, painful to themselves, to be heard, and are not always successful'. But another idea had begun to germinate in his mind, that of perpetual intercession. He proposed to begin by the institution of occasional days of intercession, and was supported in this plan by several missionary societies who had asked for the use of the church on those days. He envisaged an altar at the east end of the north aisle, and a prayer desk placed just below its steps. 'If the sacrifice of ceaseless prayer is ever to rise, even for single days, from All Saints', there must be a corner and an altar to which the merely curious do not go'.[2] He then went on to describe his vision of the altar: 'It is St Mary Magdalene's Day, and I have just offered the Holy Sacrifice in a chapel crowded with penitents. As I write, a vision of the altar of my hopes rises before me. The low oblong reredos, behind which glimpses of window, organ and sanctuary appear, is of the finest alabaster, delicately wrought in full relief and richly guilded. In the centre sits the Blessed Mother enthroned, herself enthroning the Incarnate Word who bestows His blessing on priest and people. On one side kneels St Mary Magdalene, and on the other St Mary of Egypt.'

He appealed for donations to enable this plan to be put into effect, and within a few days the appeal was answered by two members of the congregation, Mrs Swinburne and Miss Marcon, who agreed, jointly, to fund the construction of the new altar. The work was put in hand together with the cleaning and restoration of the east wall and chancel by the church architect, Ninian Comper. It took three years to complete the scheme, the whole being dedicated during the All Saints' Festival 1911.

Mackay also intended the altar to form the centrepiece of his proposed Confraternity of Prayer as part of his Campaign for the Conversion of England, inaugurated during 1911. Although these organisations no longer exist, the oak prayer bench made for this altar still bears the holder for the clock used to time prayer watches.

It was in his time that All Saints' Church

achieved much of the outward ceremonial with which is familiar today, and the first indications of what was in store were not long in coming. George Holden was described as a more advanced churchman than his predecessor William Whitworth and there is little doubt that his untimely death postponed many plans that he had for raising the standard of the outward celebration of the liturgy. Henry Mackay was not long in reviving these plans. The High Celebration at 11.45 am was renamed the Solemn Eucharist, and the acolytes were given tapers; and from the beginning of Advent 1908, the use of incense was introduced at processions and the Solemn Eucharist. Holden had acquired a thurible shortly before his death and it had been used during his obsequies. Mackay now decided that the time had come to introduce it on a regular rather than an occasional basis. The views of Upton Richards and Berdmore Compton on the use of incense are not on record, but it is reasonable to assume that they would have shared the views of their successor William Whitworth, who, since he could find no trace of its use in the first Anglican Prayer Book of 1549, concluded that it was forbidden. Mackay took great trouble in outlining his reasons, drawing upon examples of its use at worship throughout the history of the Christian church, and especially the isolated examples of its use in the Church of England during the years between the Reformation and the Oxford Movement.

Mackay showed great sensitivity in the matter, remarking that those who were not 'greatly moved' by incense would still be able to attend those services at which it would not be used – namely Morning and Evening Prayer and the Sung Eucharist at 9.00 am. 'We shall take great care that our use of incense is quiet and unobtrusive, and that the restraint and dignity which characterize the service of All Saints' are not lessened in completing their symbolism. In this sense I hope I shall be making 'no change'. By a policy of 'no change' I mean an understanding to work here on Mr Holden's lines, not a refusal to carry out his intentions'.[4]

Further liturgical 'improvements' followed in succeeding years. A paschal candlestick was presented in 1912, modelled on the one at the Certosa in Pavia. In the same year a new silver cross and six candlesticks were added to the High Altar; it is said that these are hybrid, being assembled from parts of three different sets obtained on trial by Mackay. A new sanctuary carpet was added at the beginning of the First World War. Mackay had appealed for one in May 1912. 'The present carpet is very bare and thin under the celebrant's feet. He will soon be standing on the pavement'. The colour and design were carefully chosen by Comper and the carpet was specially woven in Turkey, and was paid for by the surplus from an appeal for a new missal. Two other innovations may be recorded in Mackay's time: the use of the word 'Mass', and the custom of addressing the clergy as 'Father'. In both cases, it would seem that there was a period of verbal use before that use was formalised in the pages of the Parish Paper. The 'High Celebration' at 11.45 am on Sunday morning had been restyled the 'Solemn Eucharist' by the end of 1908. Mackay began to refer to celebrations of the 'Mass' from 1911 and, from November 1913 the Solemn Eucharist was officially renamed the High Mass. For some years Mackay made the correct distinction between secular clergy, whom he described as 'the Revd Mr' and priest members of religious orders referred to as 'the Revd Fr'. In August 1915 he described his then curate, Roscow Shedden, as 'Father Shedden', and thereafter the title was applied to all clergy.

On the death of King Edward VII in 1910, who with his wife had worshipped at All Saints' when

Prince of Wales, he allowed Ninian Comper the architect and ecclesiologist to organize a spectacular Requiem Mass for the late King, complete with black hangings, royal coats of arms, and a catafalque surmounted by an imitation crown and sceptre. Similar services were held on the death of the King's widow, Queen Alexandra, in 1925, and on the death of their son, King George V, in 1936. The deaths of Popes Pius X and Benedict XV in 1914 and 1922 respectively were commemorated in the Parish

All Saints' Church, the east end, c. 1920

96

Paper, the former announcement with black edging. But that was the extent of Mackay's regard for Rome and things Roman. It is most unlikely that he gave any thought to becoming a Roman Catholic at any stage during his ministry. One of his curates, Wilfred Moor, departed for Rome in October 1915 after a three-month sabbatical and Mackay, though he was genuinely saddened by the move, showed no trace of anger. 'I pray God that since the Bishop and all of us have tried to do our best in a difficult and painful matter, there may be little bitterness. There is none in the minds of those most closely involved'. In his earliest years as Vicar he had invited the Abbot of Caldey, Dom Aelred Carlyle, to preach during the All Saints' Festival in successive years, and he must have been saddened by the secession of that community to Rome in 1913, but has left no record of his feelings.

The great event of the history of All Saints' Church during Mackay's reign was the celebration on 28 May 1909 of the Golden Jubilee of the consecration of the church. At the beginning of that year, he announced an appeal for £2500 to restore the murals on the East Wall of the church. The question of restoration had been frequently discussed during Holden's incumbency, and Mackay decided that the restoration of the paintings should be undertaken partly to celebrate the Golden Jubilee and partly as a memorial to the late Vicar. In fact, restoration, as such, proved to be impossible. The paintings, by William Dyce, had been completed in 1858, but deterioration had set in almost immediately and restoration was undertaken by Edward Armitage in 1864. By 1905 the condition of the wall had deteriorated to such an extent that further restoration was imperative. Since one restoration had already taken place, Ninian Comper decided that any further attempt would only deprive them of any value and lose what little remained of Dyce's work. Comper decided to paint copies on movable wooden panels and place them over the originals. The work, including completion of the decoration of the north and south walls on the sanctuary, took several years and the scaffolding was not finally removed until 1914.

The Jubilee itself was kept on Thursday 27 and Friday 28 May, beginning on the Thursday evening with Solemn Evensong at 8.30 pm, at which Bishop Winnington-Ingram was preacher; Solemn Eucharist on the day itself at 11.00 am; and Solemn Evensong that evening, the respective preachers being Canon Newbolt, Chancellor of Saint Paul's Cathedral, and Fr Stanton of St Alban's, Holborn. The preceding Wednesday was kept as a vigil of continual Prayer and Intercession from 6.00 am until 9.00 pm. The whole celebration was a great success. At the first Evensong, the altar was decorated with masses of pink lilies, pink gladioli and carnations, and the whole length of the chancel screen was covered with rose-coloured paeonies and pink spirae. Bearing in mind how many former bishops had condemned the Catholic revival and looked disapprovingly at the work of All Saints', the text for the Bishop's sermon was quite appropriate: 'I will not leave you comfortless, I will come to you' (John 14:18). Among those present in the congregation was the venerable figure of Fr Richard Benson, founder of the Society of St John the Evangelist, who had preached during the octave of the consecration in 1850. Shortly after the Jubilee celebrations, one of the last links with the past was broken by the death of Elizabeth Styan, a faithful worshipper at the church for more than seventy years, who had worshipped at the Margaret Chapel during the ministry of Frederick Oakeley.

The last surviving link with those far-off days was broken towards the end of Mackay's incumbency, with the death of Robert Henry Gledhill on 5 December 1931 in his 100th year. As a young boy, he had sung in Oakeley's choir, and at his death, he was the only surviving worshipper from the Chapel that had been demolished 81 years earlier.

Mackay's work at All Saints' and his development of its liturgical style indicate that he had a full appreciation of the externals of Catholic worship, but an instinctive spiritual fear of excessive ceremonial which he held firmly in check. He wanted his church to be a model of liturgical beauty but within strictly defined lines. Much of what he introduced at All Saints' had been introduced in more 'advanced' Anglican churches many years before, but he was a cautious and prudent man and was fully aware of the pernicious effect of a beautiful and elaborate Catholic liturgy on the faith of a Christian. The puritanical streak in his nature gave him a very healthy wariness of the trappings of worship. 'We can be too much absorbed with the beauty and worship of the Catholic Religion . . . while all the time but little of the spade work of conformity with the mind and purpose of Our Lord is going on in ourselves . . . What the Lord wants is less "Praise to the Holiest in the Height" . . . and more sorrow for sin, more hatred of evil, more self-denial, more self-sacrifice and consecration of the will'.[5] Francis of Assisi was one of his favourite saints, but Mackay was very much aware of how easy it was to be captivated by the joyful and happy image of Francis as the preacher to the birds and the friend of the wolf, while at the same time wanting to forget the scourging, the tears and the torture of the stigmata.

There was nothing eccentric or pioneering about Mackay's brand of Anglo-Catholicism. He was essentially normal in the best sense of the word, and he made All Saints' 'normal' and, through his considerable influence in such circles, he made

Anglo-Catholicism as normal as he could. At All Saints', he transformed it into the kind of religion that would not offend the average Englishman who was still inclined to a deep suspicion of Catholicism as something foreign and un-English. He stood very much in the line of his four predecessors in refusing to move the church too far in the direction of Rome, and there is little doubt that he saved it from the rather conceited preciousness which afflicted so many other churches at the time. When a certain priest, on interview for a job at All Saints' confessed that he felt himself to be somewhat out of place, Mackay nodded approvingly and said 'That is exactly what I want . . . we want jarring at All Saints'.'[6] He remained faithful to the Church of England and there was never any doubt in his own mind that it was the catholic Church in England, though his critical mind made him conscious of the fact that the Church of England failed to realize fully its Catholic traditions and character. Bishop Charles Gore, who spent several years living at No. 6 Margaret Street during Mackay's incumbency, once remarked 'The difference between Mackay and me is that Mackay likes the Church of England and I do not'.[7] Mackay professed a great admiration for the pioneers of the Catholic revival, such as Fathers Mackonochie, Dolling, Stanton and Wainwright, but their world was not his. He was too reserved to be a firebrand and he would never countenance the flouting of episcopal authority as a prime duty in the cause of the propagation of the Catholic Faith. His writings show that personally he favoured the introduction of Benediction, but when the move was forbidden by Bishop Winnington-Ingram, Mackay promptly, if regretfully, obeyed. Despite its failings, he remained consistently loyal to the Church of England and never regretted its comprehensiveness.

The personal life of Henry Mackay is almost a

total mystery. His two sisters, Lily and Agnes, survived him, and a brother, Gayer, died in April 1920. He made few references to his own inner life and displayed no great hunger for human friendship, though there was to suggest that he wanted and needed praise and understanding. His fastidious air, dry clipped manner, pince nez and aloof and expressionless countenance commanded a great deal of respect, but gave him a refined and rarified appearance which made close contact and friendship with him almost impossible. Those few who did come to know him remembered that he was at his happiest when in the company of children, seemingly his sole means of relaxation, and the Choir School was his greatest joy. His book, *The Message of Francis of Assisi,* was dedicated to the boys, and the high point of his week was in his study on a Sunday evening when he would read stories to the boys. He possessed a high degree of perception and could easily scent hypocrisy. Consequently the sheer simplicity and innocence of young children and their inbuilt lack of any duplicity appealed to him. He did not need to make a conscious effort to talk down to children and could carry on a perfectly normal conversation with them as though he and they were of the same age. If there was any drawback to this ideal situation, it was that he sometimes failed to remember that they were only children.

During his incumbency 'the Choir School achieved a certain fame by mounting an annual play. These productions, frequently financed by the Duke of Newcastle, were given before invited audiences on a small stage in the School buildings. Stars of the professional stage such as Ellen Terry, Violet Vanbrugh and Forbes Robertson were present, as well as a number of other distinguished guests, eminent in other fields. Many came prepared to be bored, and departed, moved and amazed by the quality of amateur Shakespeare productions. Geoffrey Heald, one of Mackay's curates, who helped to produce the plays, later said: 'I think Mackay's happiest days was when the whole company was invited to play a matinee of The Shrew at Stratford in 1926'. At that performance, a young choirboy, Laurence Olivier, played Katherine, and attracted critical acclaim.

Mackay's background and refinement gave him a lifestyle that was eccentrically impractical in some details. He was quite incapable of understanding the workings of the London bus network and, wherever he went, it was by taxi. Fuses, wires and screwdrivers were inventions of the devil, and he could not use a reading lamp if it had an unusual kind of switch. He could not light a cigarette in the open air because nobody had taught him how to shield a lighted match from the wind, and he would rather deliver a message by hand because of his dislike of the telephone.

All his awkwardness and stiffness disappeared the moment he stepped into the pulpit. Here he was at his best. His abilities were shown to their greatest extent in his famous role as a preacher. He was a supreme artist when in the pulpit, and some of this may be due to acting connections within his own family. His brother, Gayer Mackay, was a well-known actor in his day, and Henry himself was always interested in the theatre. In the pulpit he was simultaneously unemotional and intensely dramatic. 'No preacher ever more fully understood the force of the unexpected peroration'. He had little interest in theology, despite taking a First at Oxford, and was decidedly liberal in questions of dogma. He never denounced, he never made any exhortatory clarion calls to repentence, and he was never concerned to drive home conclusions, preferring to let his subjects speak for themselves. He was more of an inspired storyteller who left his hearers to act as exegetes. But there was nothing shallow or superficial about his preaching. He had the gift of holding his congregations in thrall by his ability to lift a sentence or a character from the scriptures and to expound and develop them in a most vivid way.

Despite his inability to cope with many twentieth century inventions, Mackay had a passion for being up to date, and all his sermons were lived and thought out in his own time, and rooted and grounded in the every day experience of those who heard about him. After two initial forays into the world of writing, *The Religion of the Englishman* in 1911 and *The Message of Francis of Assisi* in 1924, he wrote nothing further until his friends persuaded him to publish some of his sermons and addresses. His first attempt was *Saints and Leaders* in 1928, and books appeared thereafter at a rate of roughly two a year until 1937. The final volume, *Last Addresses*, was published posthumously. One of his most well-known books, *Assistants at the Passion,* is an attempt to set the story of the Passion in the 20th century by sketching in the stories of some of the minor, almost anonymous, figures who are mentioned fleetingly in the gospel accounts, whose counterparts are still with us today. For example, the maid who kept the door of the High Priest's Court (John 18:15–17), who questions Peter about his friendship with Christ, is portrayed as the most difficult form of hostility to Christianity – the hostility of frivolity. 'I want you to reflect that the most dangerous enemies the gospel of Christ has to contend with are not the many who deny it, nor the few who betray it, but the multitude who trifle with it'.[9] In describing the man who offered Christ a sponge on a reed, soaked in vinegar, Mackay castigated the prevalent cult of the good-natured man, the man who scorned the need for Calvary. 'Why is it that the Living Christ, the power of the Spirit, the passion of God for souls, never seize on him and rock his soul to its foundations till he cries out? Because he has quietly, silently set himself against the Christ'.[10]

In the Catholic movement at large, Mackay was a highly respected figure. He delivered addresses at the Anglo-Catholic Priests' Convention in 1921 on the subject of the Eucharist, and at the Third Anglo-Catholic Congress in 1927 on the subject of the Reserved Sacrament. On the latter occasion the audience paid him the then rare tribute of a standing ovation for several minutes. After the death of Bishop Frank Weston of Zanzibar in 1924, he was pressed by many to take on the leadership of the Anglo-Catholic movement in England. He declined, and a rather unkind rumour was spread around that he shirked responsibility. Nothing could have been further from the truth. The primary reason for Mackay's strength and ability was that he knew himself. He knew his faults and his strengths, his weaknesses, his limitations, what he was capable of doing and what was beyond him. His refusal to become what many had hoped that he might be, a wise and trusted leader of the Anglo-Catholics, was not due to any mental or spiritual laziness, nor the shirking of duty, but a perceptive awareness of his own inability to fill that difficult office. Nevertheless he delighted in offering the altar of All Saints' to the bishops and priests who attended successive Congresses from 1920 to 1933 and quite happily stood back from any major activity. But he had a quiet and effective ministry which stretched far beyond the boundaries of his own parish and had wide-reaching consequences in the movement as a whole. He founded a dining club of twelve West London incumbents who called themselves 'Friends-in-Council'. At their monthly meetings they discussed common lines of policy and it was well known that if any higher authority desired to deal with one member, it would find itself dealing with all twelve. Invitations were issued later to other groups, and from them grew the Federation of Catholic Priests and the Anglo-Catholic Congresses. He hated committees, publicity and fools, and here were further reasons why his career advanced little beyond a prebendal stall at Saint Paul's Cathedral.

There was something about the man that made those who worked for him give him every ounce of their abilities, and he always managed to bring out the best in those who worked for him. Perhaps it was the extraordinary brilliance of his vision or the depth of his spiritual counsel backed up by an enormous fund of worldly commonsense, but certainly not his practical abilities or his ability to direct. In fact he was very bad at directing. He left his staff to develop and do their own job with very little interference, believing that that was the only way to run a non-parochial church in central London – when one man's congregation walked out, another man's moved in. He rarely criticised the sermons of his curates, despite the fact that some of them were very bad, because of a deep kindness which shrank from administering such crushing blows to those newly-ordained. During particularly bad sermons, Mackay could be seen to be sitting in his stall with a glazed expression on his face, hoping that the embarrassment would be brought to a swift conclusion. Four of his curates became bishops, three of them in his lifetime; Roscow Shedden (1909–1919), Bishop of Nassau 1919–1931; Mark Carpenter-Garnier (1905–1920), Bishop of Colombo 1924–1938; Basil Simpson (1920–1922), Bishop in Kobe (1925–1940); and Edward Roberts (1931–35) successively Bishop of Malmesbury 1956–1962, Kensington 1962–1964 and Ely 1964–1977.

Many of his sermons were collected and published in the years 1928–1937 and the majority are still enjoyable and worth reading today, fifty years after his death. Time and time again he came back to the theme of personal responsibility and personal conversion of the individual Christian, and his witness to the love of God by his own example He insisted that Christians were not merely good men and women eager for service and ready for self-renunciation, they had to be definitely converted, and converted to a clear and new life of faith. Though in many ways he was a theological liberal, he was scornfully impatient of attempts to create an undogmatic religion, a vague creedless and religionless Christianity, and he described society as 'wilting and withering in agnosticism'. He placed great emphasis on the sacrament of penance, regarding it as the inevitable milestone at which everyone would arrive sooner or later in their pilgrimage.

He constantly reiterated two great assertions of the Christian revelation in his sermons. First, that all that mankind could know of the character of God he must learn from the earthly life of Christ; and second, that all that was to be learnt could be summed up in the words 'God is Love'. If Mackay is to be described as a liberal, then it is here that his liberalism is to be found. Doctrine was essential. The use of the divinely appointed sacraments was essential. But the significance of the Christian revelation was altogether missed unless it was realised that the life of Christ was the revelation of love, and this was the instinct in and behind the ceremonial and festivals of the church. Love had to prove itself not by easy daily pleasantness, nor even by persistent consideration and charming good manners, but by an imitation of the heroism of Calvary. The Christian life was not only worship and veneration. It was determined imitation.

Two books from his prolific output deserve special mention. *Saints and Leaders,* published in

1928, and *The Twelve Gates* in 1933. Both are important works in the history of the Catholic movement in the Church of England; the first because it draws out the essential principles underlying the movement from the very different lives of six of the most famous Tractarian priests in the late 19th and early 20th centuries. The second, because, in a collection of sermons, it brings out the underlying driving force behind each of the six.

Saints and Leaders contains six essays on the lives of Fathers Lowder, Dolling, Stanton and Benson, and Bishops King and Weston. Though Mackay was not a mirror image of any of them, he was a sufficiently accomplished exegete to draw out an underlying moral in each story. In the person of Charles Lowder, he saw the inspiring and controlling spirit of a true Anglo-Catholic movement – the essential thirst for souls. 'Lowder's power was simply the power of a human will entirely given to the salvation of the souls for the glory of God; that was the power with which he applied the instrument of the Catholic Religion'. In Robert Dolling he saw the passionate concern for fighting wrong and oppression on a large scale. 'A true Anglo-Catholic movement must not be content with remedying examples of evil when it finds them . . . it must seek to remedy the conditions which maintain social wrong'. In Bishop King he saw that the way to fight the battle was to see and love the best in all men. 'In teaching a man you want to give him something better than his best. To do this you must know where to met him, you must grasp what aspect of goodness is at present appealing to him, and this can only be done by sympathy, by loving what the man loves, and loving him for it'. Arthur Stanton exhibited the consecration of all the natural gifts to Jesus. 'The complete sacrifice of this man of such wonderful beauty and power to his convictions of a life-long service of God and man, brought the whole of London to his grave'. In the person of Richard Benson he saw the overwhelming importance of the religious communities as the highest vision of life. 'Its motive is a simple and absolute surrender of self with all one has or is to God, to live in close and undisturbed fellowship with Him after the example and in obedience to the counsels of His Incarnation'. Frank Weston was the example of faithfulness unto death, a faithfulness 'that must be persevering and dauntless, and not afraid to make mistakes; it must do well, suffer for it and take it patiently; to the end of a life of self-sacrifice and many disappointments, it must retain the heart of a child'.

The Twelve Gates published in 1933 was a collection of twenty-five of the sermons delivered at All Saints' during his twenty-five year ministry. In his sermon on Zacharias (Luke 1:55ff), he dwelt heavily on the periods of spiritual dryness through which many Christians have to pass and repass. He makes the important point that for anyone who is a good servant of God, there will inevitably be times of disturbance and distress. 'Only be sure that you hold fast to God . . . remember that you have seen the Father of Jesus in the face of His Son and that the vision is the wellspring of a quenchless hope'. This theme is continued in the story of the ten lepers (Luke 17:11). Mackay believed that Christians were only deceiving people by telling them that practical Christianity consisted merely in seeking to abolish war, cruelty, poverty and oppression. Such a view was the appropriation of that part of Christ's teachings that seemed most advantageous to mankind. To take this as the essence of Christianity was to mistake the fruit of the plant for its root.

Faith, for Mackay, was not to be obtained by a painstaking accumulation of the evidence for the truth of Christianity. His concern was more for the life of faith than for the academic theological foundation. 'Put all the bits of jigsaw back into their bag; they will serve for a rainy day. Concentrate entirely on Our Lord; see whether you can obey the call "Follow me"; follow Him, watch Him, hear Him, imitate Him, work for Him, and gradually you will find yourself drawn into a relationship with Him which dominates and controls all your other relationships; that is the gift of faith. Into a future life we can take nothing but character, and it is the character of Christ alone which can lead us thither'.

At the end of his ministry, Mackay was a pathetic and weary figure. Long hours in the confessional increasingly sapped his strength and contributed to a breakdown of his health. The incessant strain of the everyday life of a priest of a central London church whose congregation is constantly changing, and who has to deal with men and women who he has little chance of knowing intimately, and yet whose personal problems he is called upon to deal with, was beginning to defeat him. The irony of the situation lay in that letter to the congregation at the start of his ministry, telling them that the health of the clergy was to be an important consideration, especially since his two predecessors had died in office. Now it seemed that he was going to go the same way. For at least two years before his resignation it became clear that he was beginning to fail. 'His voice, before so clear and resonant, had become feeble . . . His power of construction had become tragically modified . . . The Church had broken the man who had served it so well'.[11] He had been too outspoken a Catholic to be offered any preferment, save a prebendal stall at Saint Paul's Cathedral in 1920, and he had seen men of lesser ability promoted to high office. By 1934 it was clear that something had to be done if Mackay was not to die in office or face an uncomfortable and difficult retirement. Through the help of his friends

Henry Mackay with three of his former curates who had become bishops: Mark Carpenter-Garnier of Colombo (Sri Lanka), Roscow Shedden of Nassau (Bahamas), and Basil Simpson of Kobe (Japan)

and the insistence of the Archbishop of Canterbury, he was offered a residentiary canonry at Gloucester Cathedral. He accepted, preached his last sermon at All Saints' in October of that year, and a few days later, left with his sisters for Gloucester. He was installed in the Cathedral, but it was too late to mean anything to him. He had developed arterio-sclerosis and his mind had begun to fail, and he managed to

110

visit the Cathedral on only one occasion after his installation. On 20 June 1935 he was compelled to resign his stall when it became clear that he would never be able to take any part in the life and work of the Cathedral, and he left the Close with his sisters for a house in the beautiful Cotswold village of Painswick, half way between Gloucester and Stroud. There he died, of a cerebral thrombosis, during the night of Low Sunday 1936. Bishop Roscow Shedden, by then retired as Bishop of Nassau, one of the best-loved of his former curates, was with him at the end, administering extreme unction and committing his body to the grave.

Henry Mackay was buried at the local cemetery on Painswick Hill, after a simple Requiem sung in the parish church by the village choir. At the burial itself, the Choir of All Saints' was present, the boys singing the hymn 'Jesu, Lover of My Soul'. A Solemn Requiem was later sung at All Saints' Church by his successor, Dom Bernard Clements, in the presence of Guy Vernon Smith, the Bishop of Willesden, in a church that was crowded long before the Mass began. The Service was preached by the Reverend Edward Arundell, who had served as curate under three vicars – Henry Mackay, George Holden and William Whitworth. 'To a singular degree, Fr Mackay represented by his austere and controlled life all that was best in the Catholic revival. Those who knew him best recognized, behind his aloofness, a tenderness, a love, a graciousness which drew them to him in closest friendship and affection. It was the joy of his friends and the despair of his acquaintances'.[12]

Dom Bernard Clements, 6th Vicar, 1934–1941

CHAPTER SIX

THE MONK
BERNARD CLEMENTS
1934–1942

'Dom Bernard Clements I only knew
as thousands did who talked with
him now and then. Yet a brief talk with him
was no ordinary event. He came to
meet you as a friend who had no
conventional barriers to clear away.
He always kept open house, but the visitor
so welcomed knew that the springs
of his life were in the deep things of God'

(Edward Shillito in *Christ and Everyman* London,
1946, p. 7)

WILLIAM DUDLEY CLEMENTS
(DOM BERNARD CLEMENTS O.S.B.)

Born: 8 May 1880

Pembroke College, Cambridge and Trinity College, Dublin

Deacon 1908   Priest 1909

Curate of St Peter-le-Poer, Friern Barnet 1908–1911

Chaplain, Royal Navy 1911–1917

Chaplain, Training Ship Mercury 1917–1919

Vicar of St Michael and All Angels, Portsea 1919–1921

Order of Saint Benedict 1921–1942

Pershore Abbey 1921–1926

Rector of St Augustine's Theological College, Kumasi 1926–31

Nashdom Abbey 1931–1934

Vicar of All Saints', Margaret Street 1934–1942

Died: 13 September 1942

WITH the retirement of Henry Mackay after an incumbency of twenty-six years, Bishop Winnington-Ingram of London was faced with the difficulty of finding a vicar for All Saints' for the third time in his long episcopate (1901–1939). After such a long ministry, the task of finding a successor to Henry Mackay was unlikely to have been easy. His choice was bold, imaginative and unusual. The new vicar was to be Dom Bernard Clements, an Anglican Benedictine monk of the Community of Nashdom Abbey in Buckinghamshire.

William Dudley Clements was born on 8 May 1880, the eldest son of Walter Henry Clements and his wife Jeannie Mary Fabricius. Like his five predecessors, with the possible exception of Henry Mackay, very little is known of his early and private life beyond the fact that he was educated at St Andrew's School, Eastbourne and Magdalen College School, Oxford. In theory this lack of information should not be the case, since Dom Bernard was the subject of a biographical study published in 1945 under the title *Dom Bernard Clements*. The author, Edith Martha Almedingen (1898–1971) was a Russian-born historical novelist, biographer and poet of moderate obscurity, and after reading the book we find the subject a good deal more obscure. She says virtually nothing about his childhood and the book begins with his arrival as a newly-ordained curate at St Peter-le-Poer, Friern Barnet, in 1908. We are told that he had graduated from Pembroke College, Cambridge and Trinity College, Dublin (B.A. 1906), where he read Modern Literature. Of Walter Henry Clements and Jeannie Mary Fabricius we know nothing beyond the statement by Almedingen that Dom Bernard had a close relationship with his mother until her death in 1930.

After graduation, he spent several years as a schoolmaster, at St Wilfrid's Bexhill, Dunstable Grammer School and Central Foundation School, London, successively. He was ordained Deacon in 1908 and Priest in 1909, and served his title at the Church of St Peter-le-Poer, Friern Barnet, a new church, built in the suburbs of north London to replace an old church of the same name, at Old Broad Street in the City of London, demolished in 1907. Almedingen refers to 'poorly delivered and thinly spiced sermons' at this time, and his organization of a scout troop. His days as a schoolmaster and as a troop leader at Friern Barnet developed a great ministry to men and boys, though less so to women. He believed that every boy had a place in his heart for the message of Jesus Christ, if it was put fairly and squarely to him, and further that the average boy had no use for a religion that was watered down to suit modern requirements, and his blunt sincerity and 'no compromise' methods often carried the day when a more tentative approach would have ended in failure. Nothing else is known of his time at Friern Barnet.

In 1911 he entered the Royal Navy as a Naval Chaplain serving successively in *HMS Essex* 1911–1912, *Royal Arthur* 1912, *Gibraltar* 1913, *Essex* again 1914–1916, *Colossus* 1916–1917, leaving to become Chaplain of the Training Ship *Mercury* 1917–1919. Life in the Navy seemed to do him a great deal of good. It was during his days in the Navy that we have a much clearer picture of the irascible trait in his character to which he gave vent on more than one occasion. If he had any weakness, it lay in an ability to grow hot and impatient wherever he found spiritual inertia or mental slovenliness, and he often took keen pleasure in sharply minted criticisms at the expense of others.

To these dislikes may be added bureaucratic

116

inertia, and Fr Clements did battle royal with the Lords of the Admiralty on several occasions in an effort to get them to improve spiritual provision on board ships. The lack of provision of time for celebrating Mass was one of his chief complaints '. . . the Lords of the Admiralty have decided that the chief service of the Church of Christ in the Royal Navy is going to be Morning Prayer and sermon and that any other religious service is an extra, only intended for the very good, of whom there are not enough for it to be worthwhile making special arrangements . . . They call this Christian England, and in Christian England's Navy there are sometimes weary and lonely souls that yield to vice for lack of the Bread whereof a man shall eat and not die . . . How is it that when . . . several thousand men and boys are being deprived of the Body and Blood of Christ, everybody seems to keep silent . . .'[1] and he recalled the days of Henry V before the Battle of Agincourt when the soldiers of his army had confessed their sins and received the Body of Christ before they went out to do battle. Even if the Admiralty were not prepared to move on the matter, Fr Clements was, and he instituted a daily Mass while serving on *HMS Essex*, and founded a maritime servers' guild at the same time.

His naval travels took him back and forth across the Atlantic, to Madeira, Jamaica, Mexico, Cuba, Bermuda and Canada, from ship to ship, and his captains always testified to their zealous and hardworking chaplain who made a serious and determined effort to get to know the ship's company. It was quite usual for him to forgo dinner in the ward room on most nights of the week, in order to spend time visiting and talking with the ratings on the lower decks. He was released from the Royal Navy in 1917 to undertake the Chaplaincy of the Training Ship *Mercury* at Hamble under the commandership of C.

B. Fry. His work with the boys of the training ship lasted only two years until 1919, when he was appointed Vicar of St Michael and All Angels, Portsea, where he remained until 1921.

This parish was an obvious choice since it was populated largely by those who made their living from the sea, and all the various businesses connected with seafaring. Almost at once the new Vicar transformed the Vicarage into an open house for anyone who cared to call. One of his curates from those days later recalled that dinner on Saturday evening was a great affair and it was quite usual for somewhere between 25 and 30 people to sit down to a meal, all, including domestic staff, at the same table. It was not unknown for the Vicar to be seen scouring a saucepan in the scullery or flinging a dishcloth at a naval officer or some inarticulate dockhand. All who called in for a meal were made welcome, whatever their rank, but everybody was expected to lend a hand at the washing up afterwards.

In 1921 he took the decision to leave Portsea and test his vocation in the Benedictine community of Pershore Abbey. The decision was made with some difficulty, but was one that he never regretted. In view of the fact that he could be short-tempered and impatient, his decision is somewhat surprising. The two years he spent at Portsea were the only years in his ordained life in which he had complete independence to do more or less as he liked. Eleven years of obedience, first to the Vicar of St Peter's, and then to successive naval captains might have dissuaded a lesser man from losing his freedom of action after such a short space of time, and exchanging it for the strict discipline of a monastery. He was over forty years old, tempestuous and impulsive, and had taken a decision whereby his field of initiative would be greatly reduced and he would have to live in a rigidly prescribed manner. The thought in his mind that had led him to make this decision went back many years, and those around him recalled that they had long felt him to have a vocation to the religious life. He had acquired the services of Dom Denys Prideaux, the Abbot of Pershore, as his confessor, and many letters must have passed between them in the period shortly before his admission to the noviciate. Whatever the reason for his desire to enter the religious life, one of his friends later recorded his remark that 'the highest form of free will is that which results from an absolute submission to a higher authority or will'. During his time at Portsea, or perhaps even earlier, he had come to the growing realization that the highest paid service to God could not be rendered except in absolute freedom and that he was face to face with the paradox that absolute freedom was inaccessible except through absolute obedience.

The beginning of his monastic life at Pershore, where he took the name Bernard, was not easy, but he was man enough to admit the problems, many of which were caused by his own temperament, and which eventually he overcame. 'This last two or three days all my old temptations to be irritable and overbearing have come back, and I know I have been a burden at times to those around me, and I have said things deliberately to hurt people . . . I've been very bad-tempered and fussy all day'.[2] One of his fellow monks, Dom Michael Warner, later remarked 'A monastery is not a home of saints, but a school or family of souls who are trying to become holy, and therefore they often fall and make mistakes, and Dom Bernard was no exception'.[3] Towards the end of his noviciate Dom Bernard's prayer was that God would 'So hammer me into shape that He would have me'. Eventually he was solemnly professed on 11 January 1923 and decided that he wanted nothing more than to live the life of a monk, carefully dividing his life between work and prayer. But the Abbot and the Chapter were quick to recognize his obvious gifts. He had already been acting as Novice Master, and on 22 May he was appointed the first Claustral Prior, which office he held until his departure for Africa in 1926.

Although his sermons were not powerfully charged with rhetoric and brilliance, he could speak simply and directly and with such conviction that his appeal was electric. Gradually, with the approval of the Abbot, he began the round of preaching engagements and retreats, longing all the time to return to Pershore. 'I'm not really happy for more than a few days away from all that Pershore has come to mean to me, even though I get as weary as you do sometimes. Quaint discontented creatures we are, aren't we?'.[4]

There are many amusing stories about his abruptness and impatience. One will suffice. Dom Bernard was on a preaching engagement at a parish church, and on leaving the church met one of the congregation at the door. The conversation developed as follows:

Parishioner: 'Father, I've so much wanted to shake you by the hand'.

Dom Bernard: 'Take this one, I gave it a special scrub this morning'.

Parishioner: 'Your sermon was marvellous, and I know you are very busy, and I know I am not unselfish, but . . .'

Dom Bernard: 'I know you are not, and why waste time telling me about it'.[5]

He found himself spending less and less time at the Abbey, and in one way, by his sheer physical size (he was well over six feet tall) and personality, he did much to ensure a friendly disposition towards the nascent Benedictine community at Pershore. The Abbey had been founded after the Caldey debacle of

1913, when the flourishing if idiosyncratic Anglican Benedictine monastery on Caldey Island off the coast of Pembrokeshire had been received into the Roman Catholic Church after a dispute with their Visitor-Designate, Bishop Charles Gore of Oxford. A small handful of monks chose not to pursue the path to Rome and in the following year they reconstituted themselves as a new foundation at the Abbey House at Pershore in Worcestershire.

Although the earliest religious communities in the Church of England had been re-established some eighty years before, considerable suspicion still existed in certain quarters about a form of life which many believed to have been ejected from their Church at the Reformation, for reasons which they never fully understood but were nonetheless right. He endured many ill-mannered taunts and jibes from those who said he had no right to wear a habit, nor to use the letters OSB after his name. He was accused on the one side of a gross betrayal of the Anglican tradition, and on the other of 'wearing a badly cut Catholic cloak'. The complaints were directed, not so much against the fact that he was a monk, as against the very distinctive brand of Catholic Anglicanism that he taught. It would appear that he had little devotion to the use of the Rosary or to the Sacred Heart. Nor did he care much for the English Missal which was considered de rigeur in Anglo-Catholic churches of his day. He read the office from a Latin Breviary, not because he was a 'Romanist', but because the Church of England made slender provision for the needs of a Benedictine monk in the 1920s. But he always stressed the primary importance of fundamental truths, and made a sharp distinction between what was material and what was trivial. It was said of him that he would have gone to the stake in his defence of the Nicene Creed, but not for the right to wear a chasuble. He took the view that the

Communion Service in the Book of Common Prayer was the Mass and was constructed by those whose loyalty to essential Catholic principles could not be questioned without endangering the whole position of the English Church.

As with all his predecessors at All Saints', his defence of the Church of England was never in question. 'If I had been born in the Church of Rome, I should be very happy about it and should have no inclination to join the Church of England. But . . . I was born in the Church of England. I believe her to be part of the Catholic Church. If I didn't believe that, I should leave her. Being in her and observing how during the last two or three hundred years she has ceased to a good extent to use (though she possesses them) the Catholic privileges . . . I hold so dear, I believe [I am] called by God to help bring her back to them, and not run away from her because it is difficult'.[6]

The years immediately after Dom Bernard's profession proved him to be an excellent teacher and preacher. In many ways he was much like Henry Mackay (for whom he preached at All Saints' on a number of occasions) in that he possessed an outstanding ability to understand people on whatever social level and at whatever stage of a spiritual journey they might be. He had a gift for communicating the Christian faith in a way that made it seem infinitely attractive to his hearers, and also the only way forward. He could 'earth' Christianity in a way that satisfied the spiritual hunger and thirst of those who shrank from committing themselves to total acceptance of all Christian doctrine because of any kind of doubt or fear. But there was nothing anti-dogmatic about Dom Bernard, the man who had fought battles with the Admiralty over the right to celebrate the Mass on board ships of the Royal Navy; and who had given up a very promising career as a secular priest for the quite unpromising career of monasticism. If he differed from Mackay then it was because he possessed none of the clipped severity and aloofness that stemmed from Mackay's innate shyness. Being of enormous (physical) stature, shyness was not something that he could really afford.

He was made Novice Master at Nashdom, and there he would have contentedly remained, but for the fact that his superiors recognized and used his gifts to the full. The quiet periods at Pershore that he loved so much lessened as the hectic round of preaching and the conducting of retreats increased. Engagements were made further and further ahead, and, in October 1925, he wrote to his mother that he had just accepted an invitation to preach in the chapel at Tonbridge School on Suday evenings during Advent 1926.

As matters turned out, Dom Bernard was not able to keep that arrangement for the very good reason that he was sent to the Gold Coast in September 1926 to be Rector of St Augustine's College, Kumasi, a seminary for the training of African priests in the Diocese of Accra. Bishop O'Rorke of Accra had visited Pershore in 1922 and explained his plans for opening a daughter house in Kumasi. It was not intended to be a source of missionary priests who would maintain an itinerant ministry about the diocese, but a genuine attempt to found a Religious House of the Benedictine tradition, in an African setting. This was to go hand in hand with the seminary. The venture made a promising start, but, with the death of the Bishop in 1924, the plan began to falter. His successor preferred to use two monks as parish priests, and the third to run the seminary. This meant the practical disappearance of community life, and, by 1931, the Abbot decided that there was little justification for the brethren to remain in Kumasi and recalled them to England. The five years that Dom

Bernard spent as Rector of St Augustine's (1926–1931) were one of the happiest periods of his life. He took the Africans to his heart, and they reciprocated.

When he left in 1931, there was deep regret on both sides. For many years afterwards he played host to a succession of African students visiting England. He was also quite unable to use a bed again, preferring to continue his African habit of sleeping on the floor. The College survived his departure by a year, the Bishop preferring that ordinands should live at his own house. Dom Bernard's period in Africa is dealt with by Almedingen, and there is a small booklet of reminiscences and anecdotes by George Laing entitled *Dom Bernard Clements in Africa*, published in 1944. His years there are outside the scope of this book, but a few stories are worth recording. He was on good terms with almost everybody in the Gold Coast Colony, as it then was, including the Methodist missionaries from Weslyan College, the Roman Catholic Prefect Apostolic of the Northern Territory, the Chief Commissioner of Ashanti, and the King of the Ashanti, Prempeh I. He was quite convinced that racial prejudice was sinful, and the smallest arrogant gesture of a European towards an African provoked his intense anger. 'It is a stupidity as well as a sin', he once shouted at a white woman who criticised his 'familiarity' with the people of Kumasi. 'I have a crusade against all the saints' statues being made to look as if they were Englishmen', he once said, and on 17 April 1931, at a great farewell dinner for him, he expressed the hope that should he ever return to Africa, 'I beg you do not let me forget that I come as a slave to Our Lord's African children'.[7]

He was very reluctant to leave Africa and said that he would leave 'only if I am finally and decisively ordered to return to England by Father Abbot, I must, of course, go, as quite deliberately and

124

believing it to be God's will; I put myself under a vow of obedience, and I have no intention of breaking it'. Some thought that his recall to England was one of the greatest blunders every made in the history of missionary endeavours, and Almedingen described it as sheer idiocy. This was not so. Abbot Denys was right in realizing that the plan of founding a new religious house in Africa had not been realized for various reasons and there was little point in his monks being used as missionary priests.

When Dom Bernard returned to England, it was not to Pershore but to the new Abbey at Nashdom. By 1923 the community had begun to expand in a way which looked to be permanent, and the small Abbey House at Pershore would not be large enough to accommodate comfortably the growing community. Eventually the Order purchased Nashdom, a large country house, barely twenty years old, at Burnham in Buckinghamshire, and the community moved there in September 1926, almost at the same time as Dom Bernard departed for Africa. It was to Nashdom that he returned in 1931. Return is in some ways a misnomer, since he spent precious little time at the Abbey. He continued to be a widely sought-after preacher, confessor and retreat conductor and could only manage to escape to Nashdom for a few days' rest at a time. He began to broadcast during this period, and his informal style became popular. His congregation increased from hundreds to millions, and his postbag reached formidable proportions.

Dom Bernard became a very well known figure indeed in the Church of England in the years 1931 to 1934. His sane, sensible simplicity formerly delivered from the pulpit to a few and now, through the medium of the wireless, to unimaginably large congregations, brought him great fame, though he himself would have been the first to deprecate the fact. It was probably during this period that he came to the notice of Bishop Winnington-Ingram. When Henry Mackay moved to Gloucester in 1934, the Bishop offered the benefice to Dom Bernard. To his great credit, Dom Bernard replied that he was a man under authority and could not accept without the approval of his Abbot and Chapter. 'All Saints' is commonly regarded as the leading church of the whole Anglo-Catholic movement in England . . . and I felt that if I have to go to such a job it would be better to go under obedience than to choose it for myself, and so I left the decision entirely to the Community'.[8] It proved to be one of the last and best decisions of Abbot Denys Prideaux. After several years of failing health, the first Abbot of Pershore and Nashdom died a month later on 29 November 1934.

The appointment of Dom Bernard to All Saints' was received with a great deal of prejudice in certain predictable quarters. The Bishop was besieged with letters of protest, most of the writers maintaining that the appointment could not be legal because of Dom Bernard's monastic status. 'Allusions were made to a gross betrayal of the Anglican position, as if Dom Bernard were to be given a parish where the north end position and a black scarf were accepted as normal details of the Sunday observance'. Attacks were made on Dom Bernard personally, on his community, and on the monastic vocation, but he showed little concern beyond a brief reference in the Parish Paper for January 1935 to a 'difficult time of waiting', before his induction. The day of induction approached with a good deal of nervousness on the part of those closely involved. So strongly were the fears of angry demonstrations outside or maybe even inside the church, that admission was by ticket only, and police were on duty outside to prevent any trouble. In the event there were no demonstrations and the service proceeded peacefully. Much of the angry protest died down within a very short space of time, partly for the sheer lack of any kind of substance in the objections, and partly because of the very sensible decision on the part of the Bishop and others to ignore them.

The beginning of his ministry was not easy. Dom Bernard found it difficult to exchange the warmth of community life for the inevitable loneliness of the life of a celibate parish priest. Looking back at the situation, it would have seemed sensible to second one, or perhaps two, other members of the community on a permanent basis to act as his curates and thereby maintain some semblance of the monastic life to which Dom Bernard had felt himself to be called. No doubt there were good reasons at the time for not pursuing such a course. There were other minor problems such as the difficulty he experienced in accommodating his enormous figure to the small sanctuary and polished precision of the ceremonial of All Saints'. Many members of the congregation had known only Henry Mackay as their Vicar, and the appearance of this gigantic monk was quite alarming to some of them. The old enemy finance reared its ugly head yet again at the beginning of his ministry, and not for the first time did an incoming Vicar of All Saints' find himself inheriting a church that was in debt, this time to the amount of £583. Yet again an appeal was launched, and yet again the congregation responded generously to ensure that the new vicariate should be able to clear past debts as quickly as possible. By the beginning of March the deficit had been reduced to £75. In the Parish Paper for April, the new Vicar appealed for new sets of vestments to replace the large number which had belonged personally to Mackay and which had departed with him to Gloucester.

Despite these early minor difficulties, Dom Bernard now had a London base from which he could exercise his increasingly potent personal ministry to the many who sought his guidance. He had the support of four curates, which might sound excessive until we point out that the geographical parish of All Saints' was still largely residential in 1934, and not the weekend desert that it is fifty years later. People still lived in Mortimer Street, and there were troops of cubs, scouts and guides, who were taken on camping trips to Brittany. The Choir School was thriving, and it gave as much pleasure to Dom Bernard as it had given to his predecessor. In 1935 the boys were taken for a day's outing to Nashdom, where they thoroughly enjoyed themselves, finishing the day by singing in the Abbey Chapel. Dom Bernard never forgot that he was still a monk and a man under authority and he tried to spend most of August each year in residence at Nashdom. One of his first visiting preachers was Dom Martin Collett, the new Abbot. Their relationship was perhaps not as warm as that which had existed between Dom Bernard and Abbot Denys, but the former always remembered his vow of obedience and when the Abbot paid his periodic visits to All Saints' Dom Bernard obediently got down on his knees and kissed the Abbot's ring. When Dom Martin first preached, on 14 July 1935, he prefaced his sermon with an appeal which might have been better received in 1935 than it would now. 'As you have just heard, your alms at this Mass are to be given to Nashdom Abbey. Perhaps I may be allowed to say to you that our loan . . . of Dom Bernard to be Vicar of this church has involved us in a quite considerable financial loss; and that, whereas income was previously none too large for the needs of the Community, it is now too small; and I have confidence that you will not let Dom Bernard's home suffer on your account'.[9]

Although this initial deficit was quickly cleared, money has always been a problem at All Saints', and Dom Bernard's time was no exception. Other debts took the place of the first and, although he reported in the Parish Paper for January 1936 that yet another deficit – 'this unpleasant beast', as he called it – 'had expired', he was forced to appeal in the following month for money to increase his own stipend. He told that congregation that a secretary was an absolute necessity. He received an average of thirty letters a day, a figure which sometimes rose to seventy-seven after a broadcast. 'If everyone of the Communicants' Roll were to pay in annually in January either 10s or £1 the matter would be more than comfortably settled, and then the Easter Offering would really be a happy gift, and not an essential part of one's income, the amount of which one waits to hear with strained anxiety!'.[10]

The year 1936 saw the Golden Jubilee of the Parish Paper, founded by William Whitworth in November 1886, and among the articles was one by Fr Cyril Whitworth SSJE, one of his four sons. But the climax of anniversaries came in 1939 with the centenary of the licensing of Frederick Oakeley as Minister of Margaret Chapel on 5 July 1839. It was an occasion not to be forgotten. The programme was as follows:

Tuesday 4 July
6 pm   Solemn Evensong, Sermon and Procession
        Preacher: The Dean of St Paul's Cathedral

Wednesday 5 July
11 am High Mass of the Blessed Trinity
        Preacher: The Vicar

  6 pm Solemn Evensong, Sermon and Procession
        Preacher: The Reverend Michael Newbolt,
        Canon of Chester

Thursday 6 July
11 am High Mass of the Blessed Sacrament
  6 pm Solemn Evensong and Sermon
      Preacher: The Dean of Manchester

Friday 7 July
11 am High Mass of the Passion
  6 pm Solemn Evensong and Sermon
      Preacher: The Reverend Gerald Vernon,
      Rector of Christ Church, St Leonards-on-Sea

Saturday 8 July
11 am High Mass of Requiem
      Preacher: The Archdeacon of Cornwall
  6 pm Solemn Evensong and Sermon
      Preacher: The Bishop of Willesden

Sunday 9 July
11 am High Mass in the Octave
      Preacher: The Archbishop of York
  6 pm Solemn Evensong, Sermon and Procession
      Preacher: The Archbishop of Wales

Monday 10 July
11 am High Mass of the Propagation of the Faith
  6 pm Solemn Evensong and Sermon
      Preacher: Canon Maurice Gillson, Vicar of All
      Saints', Clifton

Tuesday 11 July
11 am High Mass of the Holy Angels
  6 pm Solemn Evensong (No sermon)

Wednesday 12 July
11 am High Mass of the Holy Ghost
      Preacher: The Reverend John Hooper, Rector
      of Kenn
  8 pm Solemn Evensong, Sermon and Procession
      Preacher: The Bishop of Argyll and the Isles

On the centenary day itself, Bishop Winnington-Ingram, who had announced his impending retirement, was present in the sanctuary and at the lunch held afterwards at the Café Royal in Regent Street, attended by nearly 300 people, including seven bishops.

The Archbishop of Canterbury, Cosmo Gordon Lang, had been invited to preach, but owing to commitments was unable to be present for the centenary week. He did agree to preach on November 8, the octave of All Saints' Day, at Solemn Evensong. It was only the second occasion on which an Archbishop of Canterbury had preached at All Saints', the first being the visit of Archbishop Benson on Ascension Day in 1886. On the Sunday preceding the beginning of the centenary celebrations, Evensong was broadcast from All Saints' as a way of bringing the celebrations to the notice of a wider congregation, and Dom Bernard preached a sermon in which he praised the work of the church in Margaret Street over the past hundred years, naturally extolling the beauty of the liturgy and the music, but, like all his predecessors and successors, delivering a veiled warning to his hearers not to be carried away by such things. 'The music, the beauty, were to be the outward expression of the principles of the Catholic Revival. But the bedrock principle of the Catholic Revival was the fact that the Christian soul is not only in intimate personal relationship with a God who loves it and died for it, but that it is, as St Paul taught us, by its Baptism an actual living part of the Body of Christ, its Lord – so that it is not the soul that lives, but Christ living in the soul. All the beauty and the music come from that. All our joy comes from that. All our sacraments are that truth expressing itself. That is the explanation without which so many people miss what we are at – we who glory in the name of Catholic'.[11] Again, like so many other priests at All Saints', Dom Bernard was very quick to pour scorn on the lace-edged fussiness about liturgical details. 'There are a fair number of people who are intensely interested in the details of worship. They always know whether the priest's chasuble is too short, or whether one of the servers took a wrong turning during the Offertory, but of the Mass itself they may not know very much'.[12]

The centenary in 1939 was the zenith of Dom Bernard's ministry at All Saints' because, less than two months later, the Second World War began, and life at the church was radically changed. The future of the Choir School hung in the balance, and, at one point, Dom Bernard issued an ultimatum to the congregation. The Choir School was almost bankrupt, and unless £500 was forthcoming from the congregation within seven days, the school would close at the end of the following week. Even the Archbishop of Canterbury, on his visit to All Saints' in November, remarked that closure would be a tragedy for the whole Church. The money appeared. Many people at the time thought that the Choir School had no future but the Vicar thought otherwise and fought for its future. Like many other children in London, the boys were evacuated to the countryside, first to Sussex and later to Freeland near Oxford.

Although the Church was spared serious damage in the Blitz, the nerves of its clergy were not. The congregation dwindled and services were curtailed, and a voluntary choir was formed, including ladies who had to sit out of sight! On one day, the only service was a Mass said privately in the Vicar's study. After one particular heavy bombing raid, Dom Bernard wrote to the Headmaster of the Choir School at Freeland saying that the Vicarage was 'still full of ash and muck . . . [Yet] what we have tried to build is not in bricks and mortar and things of material beauty, and we come back to "Fear not them that can kill the body but after that have not more that they can do". I can't always remember it in moments of stress, and I am a very great coward physically . . . I only ask you to pray that my feelings of fear may not be allowed to hinder me from doing the things Our Lord would have me do'.[13] He was very worried about the future and safety of the Church, and the anxiety only increased when the roof of No. 84 Margaret Street, the Parish School, was set on fire by an incendiary bomb. There is a story that so violently did he dislike the stained glass windows in the baptistry that he completed their destruction after partial damage by bomb blast.

The summer of 1941 brought a brief respite from the bombing, but Dom Bernard's work increased considerably. His broadcasting commitments grew heavier, in particular live broadcasts to the people of Malta every Sunday for nearly a year. During that same summer the Headmaster of the Choir School fell seriously ill and, failing to find a replacement, Dom Bernard undertook to teach the boys himself. We wonder how he managed to maintain such a punishing schedule, spending the weekends in London, or away on preaching engagements, and the weekdays in Oxford.

Sooner or later the strain was bound to tell, and in the summer of 1942 Dom Bernard felt tired enough to admit the fact. He agreed to take a proper holiday, instead of the odd day here and there since 1939. He went down to St Mawes in Cornwall, intending to remain on leave until 15 September. From St Mawes he travelled to Lelant, and there he fell ill and died from appendicitis, on 13 September. After a requiem at All Saints', his body was taken back to Nashdom for burial.

When the matter of a permanent memorial to Dom Bernard at All Saints' was considered, the family asked that he should be depicted as he had lived, so the small brass in the chancel floor shows him in monastic habit and wearing spectacles. It is a unique combination in such a medium.

Without doubt, Dom Bernard was a spiritual, as well as a physical giant, and any attempt to describe this 'great' man more than forty years after his death is likely to be inadequate. We have already mentioned the poverty of Almedingen's biography. But this was corrected by an appreciation of Dom Bernard written in 1945 by Fr Leslie Simmonds, his curate from 1936 to 1941. He criticised the intruded comments of the authoress, of which there are many, and which obscure the subject. She concentrated largely upon his devotion to the Choir School but not at all upon his far-reaching work of spiritual direction and in the confessional; his Wednesday Lenten mission services which filled the church; and his interest in and visits to the University hostels.

Those who knew Dom Bernard have described him as 'hilariously funny and very holy' and 'sanctified by common sense'. He was meticulous in his friendships, extremely loyal to his staff and had no favourites. He disliked sloppiness and slipshod ways and sheer laziness, but he could always recognize and care for human frailty, and nobody at All Saints' ever heard his voice raised in anger. He had a good sense of humour and was quite capable of poking fun at himself and his enormous bulk. Because of his size, a new bath, since removed, had to be installed in the Vicarage. So large was it that Dom Bernard would always joke that the parish boundary ran through his bath. On one occasion a parishioner offered to drive him in her car to a lunch that they were both to attend. The car proved to be a Baby Fiat. 'It was one of the many dramatic moments outside the Vicarage to see him inserting himself . . . Fortunately it was summer so the sunshine roof was open. Dom Bernard was quite unperturbed and said "Just leave it to me to manage. A shoe horn will not be needed".'[14] When

134

Dom Bernard Clements in Africa

staying with his sister in Eastbourne, he went on the pier and weighed himself on one of those machines which, instead of issuing a card, spoke your weight. When his twenty or so stone was announced, a Yorkshire voice behind him remarked: 'Eh bah goom, that's a man's weight that is'.

The fullest answer to Dom Bernard's great power and ability lay in his intense interest in every person with whom he came into contact. He could make someone realize that they mattered a great deal to him. Everybody was important and he really did care about the salvation of souls in a way which made those who heard him see that salvation was something very wonderful. He knew how to identify himself with his audience. 'He was not a great orator in the sense of being a producer of resounding, perfectly worded sentences, nor was he a subtle logician, though always clear in his sequence of thought'.[15] His sermons, of which a selection were published in sixteen books between 1929 and 1946, have lost some of their force in print, unlike those of Fr Mackay which are still in the main very readable. But this is not because Dom Bernard was a bad preacher. Mackay delivered beautifully polished discourses which could be read and re-read without losing much of their colour and interest. Dom Bernard's sermons were intended for the people sitting in front of him, not necessarily for future readers. When he spoke to an audience, he felt the pulse and needs of that audience and spoke to them alone. 'His hearers thought with him because he appeared to be thinking with them'.[16] This personal identification arose because he himself was intensely aware of the unity of all believers in the mystical Body of Christ, and it was summed up in a letter he wrote to one of his African students on leaving Kumasi in 1931. 'And now we are not to be sad, because we are all living parts, you and I, of the wonderful Body of Christ, of which we have often thought together in these past five years, and if He chooses to use one of His hands, which is me, in Europe, at the same time that he is using another one of his hands, which is you, in Africa, there is nothing in that to be sad about, any more than a man need be sad because one of his hands is holding a piece of bread and butter while the other hand is doing a totally different work of trying to open a door'.[17]

Dom Bernard was survived by his sister, Violet, who died, unmarried, in 1943.

CHAPTER SEVEN

THE SHOWMAN
CYRIL TOMKINSON
1943–1951

*'Beyond his mannerisms there was an
immense love of God and a great
compassion for human beings . . .
He was never content to stay long in one
place. His darting movements were
outward and visible signs of a personal
restlessness. It was as if he was always
actively wanting to know more of the
loving purposes of God'*

(Bishop Wilfrid Westall writing in the *Church Times*
on 14 June 1968)

Cyril Tomkinson, 7th Vicar, 1943–1951 (centre right) with the boys of the Choir School

CYRIL EDRIC TOMKINSON

Born: 15 May 1886

Sidney Sussex College, Cambridge 1905–1910

Wells Theological College 1910

Deacon 1910   Priest 1911

Curate of St Thomas with St Saviour, Southwark
1910–1912

Permission to Officiate, Diocese of Exeter 1912–1913

Curate of St Stephen, Bournemouth 1913–1915

Permission to Officiate, Diocese of Exeter 1915–1918

Curate of St Stephen, Bournemouth 1918–1923

Curate of St Mary the Less, Cambridge 1923–1930

Vicar of St Stephen's, Lewisham 1930–1934

Vicar of St Bartholomew's, Brighton 1934–1937

Permission to Officiate, Dioceses of London and
Bath & Wells 1938–1939

Vicar of All Saints', Clifton 1939–1943

Vicar of All Saints', Margaret Street 1943–1951

Permission to Officiate, Diocese of Canterbury
1951–1952

Permission to Officiate, Diocese of Chichester
1952–1953

Chaplain of St Edward's House, West Malvern
1953–1954

Died: 5 June 1968

ON the death of Dom Bernard, the task facing Geoffrey Francis Fisher, the new Bishop of London, was as difficult as that which had faced Bishop Winnington-Ingram on the retirement of Fr Mackay in 1934, and he reacted as wisely as his predecessor in his choice of a new Vicar for All Saints'. Dom Bernard's ministry was unique, based largely upon his own personality and spirituality, and there could be no question of seeking an identical successor. The appointment of somebody similar who would, inevitably, prove to be a faint carbon copy, would do nothing to ensure the future of the church. The war really put an end to All Saints' as a parish church by depopulating its parish through bombing and evacuation. The beginning of the decline had been evident before the war, which only speeded up the process. The task of appointing an incumbent to a church whose congregation is entirely non-resident, is not easy, especially in central London, with a great and diverse choice of churches within easy reach of each other. It would be quite easy for a congregation to express its displeasure of a new incumbent by voting with its feet and walking out – to the next-door church if need be. This need not be a problem if the new man has a character strong enough to gather around him a new congregation. But an attempt to find somebody 'like' the former incumbent would be doomed to failure.

Geoffrey Fisher understood this point perfectly when he appointed Cyril Edric Tomkinson as the seventh Vicar of All Saints', Margaret Street.

Cyril Tomkinson was born on 15 May 1886, the second son of Frederick Tomkinson, of the firm of stockbrokers of the same name. The family lived in the prosperous area of Upper Norwood, now part of the London Borough of Croydon. He had an elder brother, Herbert, who also became a priest, though of lower churchmanship, and ended his days as Vicar

140

of Hove; a younger brother, Lancelot, who joined the Navy and of whom he was very fond; and a sister, Eva, who died early in the 1920s. He was educated at Dulwich College and at Sidney Sussex College, Cambridge, from where he graduated in Classics and Theology in 1910. After a brief period at Wells Theological College, he was ordained deacon in 1910 and priest the following year, by the Bishop of Southwark, and served his title at the Church of St Thomas with St Saviour, Southwark. He remained there only two years before leaving for the Diocese of Exeter, where he is recorded as having been granted 'Permission to Officiate'. His short stay at Southwark, and an unidentified period of work in Exeter were the first signs of a career which was to be marked by restlessness. His eight-year ministry at All Saints', which was his final appointment before retirement, was the longest of any of the jobs that he held during his career. Southwark was followed by two seven-year curacies – at St Stephen's, Bournemouth and at St Mary the Less, Cambridge, respectively – and it was not until 1930, at the age of forty-four, that he became an incumbent for the first time, on his appointment as Vicar of St Stephen's, Lewisham. He stayed there for four years before moving to St Bartholomew's, Brighton. He left there in 1937 and, after a two-year gap, during which he was given 'Permission to Officiate' in the Dioceses of London and Bath and Wells, he was appointed to the living of All Saints', Clifton in Bristol. It was from there that he was called by Geoffrey Fisher to succeed Dom Bernard as Vicar of All Saints' in 1943.

The arrival of Cyril Tomkinson in 1943 must have been a great shock to the congregation of All Saints', if only for the fact that he was quite unlike Dom Bernard in physical appearance. Whereas the latter was a physical giant standing well over six feet tall, Cyril Tomkinson was hardly more than five feet.

With the exception of a small book of devotions based on the Stations of the Cross, published in 1938, he wrote nothing. This was in sharp contrast to his two immediate predecessors who published volumes of their sermons. He had something of the personal privacy of Mackay, and the irascibility of Dom Bernard, and a sense of humour which sprang from both these qualities and which was entirely his own. Those people who knew him, and who are still alive at the time of writing, recall him as a very vivid personality whose image has not faded with the passage of time. Others, who did not know him, have referred to him as the least remembered Vicar of All Saints', who did little more than a holding operation between the ministries of Dom Bernard and Kenneth Ross.

It is a great pity that so little of Cyril Tomkinson has survived, that is apart from a wealthy fund of memories, funny stories and anecdotes. From what we have heard, it would be easy to dismiss him as a man of humourous wit, but with very litle else, and with no spiritual depth. This would be a superficial picture of a man who used that superficiality to conceal both a great pastoral heart and a deep spiritual insight. What made him move around from place to place with a restlessness that might well be said to have bordered on insecurity, is a question that is largely beyond answering at this stage in time. What little we have been able to glean about his life leads us to see him as a man with a delightfully impish sense of humour who used it to the maximum effect.

Thankfully, Cyril Tomkinson has not entirely disappeared from view. In 1982, Fr Harry Williams CR, who had been his curate from 1946 to 1948, published his own autobiography in which he includes memories of his former Vicar. He described him as a 'short man in the middle fifties who, when he stood or walked, looked like a small, cheeky bird. He was able to manipulate his eyes like a born comedian so that they gave exaggerated expression to whatever feeling he wished to parody'.[1] He was very accomplished at parodying himself and exposing his own character to public humour. Coming from a family of stockbrokers, he would remind the congregation whenever he appealed for money for a parish project that he himself did not cost them anything, and when once asked about prayer he responded, 'People speak about prayer. But the only prayer I ever say is to thank God that my father was a stockbroker'.[2] The style was flippant and the content trivial, but there is an appealing frankness about this point that was typical of the man.

As with all his predecessors, his attitude to All Saints' and its liturgy and ministry was a strange mixture of healthy distrust and firm loyalty if not affection. He had little real regard for the liturgy of the Church, the Sunday theatre as he called it, but maintained it much in the style that he had inherited. It was not unknown in his day for people to travel to All Saints' from Bristol, catching the overnight sleeper on Saturday night, arriving in time to communicate at the 7 am Mass on Sunday, and staying for the non-communicating High Mass, before returning that afternoon. He regarded this behaviour as utterly ridiculous and deprecated such silliness. He was convinced that the real work at All Saints' was done during the week, either in the confessional or on the more informal basis of private counselling. Nevertheless, like Mackay, he was punctilious about ritual matters and anxious that perfection should be the guiding rule.

He was firm in his loyalty to the Church of England and would not countenance the use of any rite other than in the Book of Common Prayer. Hugh Ross Williamson, the editor, playwright, politician

143

and broadcaster, who was ordained an Anglican priest in 1943, remembered him, with Bishop William Wand of London and Dom Gregory Dix of Nashdom Abbey, as one ot the three great wits of the Church of England; "but he was a Protestant-in-chasuble par excellence and refused to allow me to say even a private Mass at All Saints – 'because, my dear, you'll use that horrid Roman book and the rule here is music by Mozart, choreography by Fortescue, decor by Comper, but' – his long forefinger wagged rougishly and his voice became solemnly emphatic – 'libretto by Cranmer'.[3] He was inclined to think that Mackay had introduced too many theatrical effects into the liturgy and was once heard to remark before the start of a High Mass, "My dear, I wonder Mackay didn't introduce make-up".[4]

There are many such stories which show him to have been the master of a powerful, naughty and humorous wit which gave him such great human warmth and endeared him to so many people. The following will give some idea of the man. During a discussion to raise money for the church:

'Couldn't we hire out opera glasses at the back of the nave?'

On an occasion when Eric Abbott (Dean of Westminster, 1959–1974) was preaching at All Saints' on the difference between the holiness of beauty and the beauty of holiness:

'Well, at least nobody ever thought I was beautiful, which is more than can be said for Eric'.

To his curate, Harry Williams, on a sermon in which he had concentrated too much on style at the expense of the content:

'You gave us quite a good meal this morning, but it was served in such elegant old silver as to be slightly cold. A miserable performance, my dear'.

On advising a couple who were planning to get married:

144

'Until the wedding you mustn't do anything which couldn't be put on the stage at the Haymarket'. On being asked about the possibility of holding coffee mornings at the church:

'I was ordained to administer the sacraments, not Nescafé!'

A Collect about John Briscoe, a well-known and spiritually haughty director of souls:

'O God who has given unto thy servant John Briscoe a proud look and high stomach, mercifully grant that as we have been chastened by the rod of his correction, so we may be aided by his condescending intercession . . .'

A Collect for fine weather at Ascot:

'. . . that the rich may glorify Thee by their clothes and think well of Thee in their hearts . . .'

On meeting the Most Reverend Geoffrey Fisher, Archbishop of Canterbury and Primate of All England, in the Athenaeum of which club they were both members:

'Evening Fisher'.

On interviewing a prospective curate:

'Are you the sort who falls in love with choirboys?'

Almost inevitably, people compared Cyril Tomkinson unfavourably with Dom Bernard and it seems that there was a certain degree of change-over in the congregation in 1943 and thereafter. Cyril rarely made any reference to his predecessor, and when he did so they were guarded ones. He stayed on at All Saints' until 1951 – a period of eight years – when he retired to live in Cambridge in his sixty-fifth year. Those who knew him at the time recall his increasing frailty and there may have been an increasing awareness on his own part that All Saints' was becoming a burden that he was no longer physically equipped to bear. He was forever complaining of ill-health, though he was always prone to hypochondria and there is no telling how ill he might have been. Administration bored him, he worried a good deal about almost everything and he was always erratic in his behaviour. There was never a regular staff meeting at All Saints'. They were only held when Cyril thought it might be a good idea. He may have felt that by 1951 the job was simply too big for him to manage.

After his resignation, he settled eventually at 54 Huntingdon Road, Cambridge, where he remained almost until the end of his life, helping at the Church of St Giles, his activity increasingly restricted by the progressively disabling Parkinson's Disease. He left Cambridge in 1967 for a nursing home near Bury St Edmunds, where he died on 5 June 1968. Always a showman to the end of his life, one of his friends recalled hurrying to Cyril's hospital bedside on hearing that he was close to death, only to find him sitting up attired in a dressing gown, waving a blessing at everyone in sight and offering glasses of sherry to his visitors.

In his will he left legacies to all the churches in which he had served, but he had always said that Little St Mary's was his favourite and his legacy to that church was twice the size of the others.

Anecdotes about Cyril Tomkinson are legion, most of them indicating a forthright sense of humour. He has been described as a roguish creature, and somebody who looked and sounded like Mr Punch. Perhaps the best assessment was made in a supplement to his obituary in the *Church Times* for 14 June 1968, by the Right Reverend Wilfrid Westall (Bishop of Crediton, 1954–1974):

'He was a devoted priest, a holy man, a wise counsellor and a great character . . . he took me under his wing and taught me much for which I have always been profoundly grateful . . . I think he secretly enjoyed the deference which was due – or

146

which he thought was due – . . . to an elderly senator
. . . He was never content to stay long in one place.
His darting movements were outward and visible
signs of a personal restlessness. It was as if he was
always actively wanting to know more of the loving
purposes of God'.[5]

Kenneth Ross, 8th Vicar, 1951–1969

CHAPTER EIGHT

THE INTELLECTUAL
KENNETH ROSS
1951–1969

'His unlimited patience, his understanding of the mixture of motives underlying all our actions, of our boundless capacity for self-deception and of the need to distinguish between sin and temptation were qualities which made him the most sought-after confessor in London'

(Margaret Hodgetts, *Kenneth Ross: the Margaret Street Years 1951–1969*, p. 36)

KENNETH NEEDHAM ROSS

Born: 28 November 1908

Merton College, Oxford 1925–1931

Cuddesdon Theological College 1931–1932

Deacon 1931   Priest 1932

Curate of St Michael and All Angels, Radford
1931–1932

Chaplain of Salisbury Theological College 1932–1936

Vice-Principal of Salisbury Theological College
1936–1941

Vicar of St John the Baptist, Old Malden 1941–1951

Vicar of All Saints', Margaret Street 1951–1969

Chancellor and Canon Residentiary of Wells
Cathedral 1969–1970

Died: 8 June 1970

150

LOOKING back at the life and work of Kenneth Needham Ross, the eighth Vicar of All Saints', we are immediately struck by the remarkable similarities between his life, and that of the fifth Vicar, Henry Mackay. Kenneth Ross was born in November 1908, six months after the induction of Henry Mackay as Vicar of All Saints'. Both men read theology at Merton College, Oxford, and both gained a First Class Honours degree, Mackay in 1887 and Ross in 1931. Both men had something of a brief academic career, Mackay as Librarian of Pusey House, Oxford, and Ross as Chaplain then Vice-Principal of Salisbury Theological College. Both men served lengthy incumbencies at All Saints', Mackay for twenty-six years and Ross for eighteen. Both men probably stayed too long in the job and retired for reasons of weariness, among others. Both men went to residentiary canonries at West Country cathedrals, Mackay to Gloucester and Ross to Wells. Both men died within two years of their departure and both were survived by their two unmarried sisters – Lily and Agnes Mackay and Constance and Marian Ross. Both men were of a shy and retiring nature who led intensely private personal lives, but who were highly polished and professional priests in public. There were certainly differences between the two men, which we shall come to later in the chapter, but their lives mirrored each other to an interesting degree.

Kenneth Needham Ross was born on 28 November 1908, the youngest child and only son of William George Ross of Worcester, and his wife Elizabeth Ann. He was devoted to his parents who were described as 'people of great charm and old-fashioned goodness'.[1] He was a scholar at King's School, Worcester, and his abilities were such that he was chosen as head of the school. It was during these years that his vocation to the priesthood was formed under the influence of Canon T. A. Lacey of Worcester Cathedral, 'a man of deep erudition, and a spiritual director of rare genius and discernment'.[2] From there he went to Merton College, Oxford, where he gained a First in Classical Moderations, a Second in Literae Humaniores, and then a First in Theology after only one year's study. It was a great achievement, though it involved a fair measure of strain, and a testimony to his able and competent mind. Part of his success was due to the influence of his friendship with Frederick Wastie Green, the Theology tutor, one of those individuals who had the rare ability to bring the subject to life and make it an exciting and stimulating academic discipline. Ross never ceased to be grateful to the influence of Green on the formation of his mind.

He went straight from Merton to a year's study at Cuddesdon Theological College, and was made a deacon at Michaelmas 1931, serving his title at the parish of St Michael and All Angels, Radford. He was ordained by Henry Mozley, Bishop of Southwell, a friend of Green. Almost as soon as he had been ordained priest, pressure was brought upon the diocese to release him for work as chaplain and tutor at Salisbury Theological College. He might have been destined for an academic career but for the fact that in 1941 he chose to leave Salisbury and accept a living in the gift of Merton College – St John the Baptist, Old Malden, in Surrey.

St John's was not a traditional Anglo-Catholic church, more 'ceremonially Anglican' as one there at the time remembered it. In the ten years that he was Vicar of the parish, Kenneth Ross made his mark on the place and is remembered fondly by those who were there at the time. One recalled him as a man with a determined approach to what he wanted to do. He suffered fools gladly, but only if they were genuine fools, and he was capable of anger, firing the occasional broadside at the Parochial Church Council. He had an aura about him which inspired awe, and a charisma of which he never seemed to be aware. He was an extraordinarily accurate judge of human nature, telling one couple who came to him for marriage preparation that they were not well suited. The point was well made because several years later they divorced. He had a way of knowing everything that was going on in the parish and often destroyed nascent cliques by carefully directed moral judgements in his sermons. During his time at Old Malden a number of excellent qualities emerged. He was liturgically knowledgeable; he was a good pastor with a respected ministry in the confessional; and he was an able preacher. Years afterwards, when asked why he had never produced a great theological work, he replied that he was not an academic, and his years in the parish proved that, despite his shyness and reserve, he was a proficient parish priest. All of which made him a natural candidate for the incumbency of All Saints' when Cyril Tomkinson retired early in 1951.

The *Church Times* greeted his appointment with enthusiasm remarking that All Saints' would receive 'a priest of distinction and capability'.[3] We presume that his reputation at that time must have come almost entirely from the qualities listed above since, during his time at Malden, he had published only two books, both of a non-theological nature. *Homes in Danger* (jointly with Percy S. Wigram) in 1945, and *A History of Malden* in 1947. During his eighteen years, he produced a large number of booklets and pamphlets of a highly populist nature, in the best sense of the term, roughly at the rate of two a year. But that was all in the future. His appointment in 1951 was greeted with little euphoria because he was so little known. In his first letter to the congregation of All Saints', he wrote of the unique position of the

Vicar of the Church, wishing that he were more worthy and more capable of shouldering the responsibility. At the service of institution and induction, Bishop William Wand of London urged the greatest possible co-operation between the people of the parish and their new priest. A not unfamiliar induction sermon.

Kenneth Ross's years at All Saints' were marked by flux and change and, although he managed to hold the church together through a difficult era, almost until the end of his ministry there, his time was one of intense personal stress, just as it had been for all his predecessors, and he left in 1969, as Henry Mackay had done in 1934, a weary and dispirited man. The whole sociological phenomenon of the 1960s coincided with great changes in the liturgy of the church, particularly after the Second Vatican Council, which sent Roman Catholic devotion and liturgy exploding in all directions. By the end of the 1960s, the liturgy of All Saints' was no longer in the vanguard of the Catholic movement in the Church of England. It was still performed with feeling and beauty, but to some extent it had been passed over by the changes in the rest of the church. His shyness and reserve were perhaps not as well received and appreciated towards the end of his ministry as they might have been at the beginning. Nevertheless, we believe from what we have read, heard and know of his ministry that possibly he was the greatest Vicar of All Saints'. He was a learned scholar who read widely and voraciously; a kind and sensitive pastor of souls; and a very holy priest. In the years to come, when the dust clouds have settled over the decisions of 1968, we hope that it may be possible for a more objective and less emotional assessment of the of Kenneth Ross.

In the preceding chapters, we have identified that common theme of strong loyalty to the Church of England that has permeated the history of All Saints', as well as being one of the common strands connecting each incumbent with his predecessor. In the case of Kenneth Ross, this theme gained a new emphasis when, in 1953, he published a 125-page book entitled *Why I am not a Roman Catholic*. It was a bold statement to come from a part of the Church of England which many of its opponents have, in the past, castigated as nothing more than a stepping stone to the Roman Catholic Church. None of his seven predecessors had gone into print on the subject. Neither have any of his successors to date, though this must be considered as unlikely in view of the improved state of ecumenism in the years since 1965. His book is a clear, succinct and well-ordered statement of his principles.

It was published in the years after the formation of the Church of South India (an amalgamation of the Anglican Church in South India with various non-episcopal churches). The scheme of unity had provided for a presbyterate composed of Anglican priests, and ministers from the uniting churches who were not required to undergo episcopal ordination. This caused great anxiety in Anglo-Catholic circles and a flurry of secessions to the Roman Catholic Church. Kenneth Ross refused to take part in any kind of a stampede and published his reasons without any feelings of antagonism towards the Roman Church. '. . . It is in no belligerent spirit that I criticize the Church of Rome. I am glad to say that I have spent more of my ministerial life defending her against wrongful attacks than attacking her myself. I would prefer humbly to seek to imitate her virtues than to parade her vices. But the Church of England is the constant target of Roman Catholic attack, not always in the best of taste, and I must defend my Mother'.[4] Ross argued that the dogmas of the Assumption and the Immaculate Conception could be held as pious opinions, were probable, and that the

155

Church of England did not require disbelief in them, but that they could be held to be necessary to salvation as Articles of Faith. He condemned papal infallibility as untrue, and upheld the Church of England as part of the Catholic Church with a valid ministry and valid sacraments. He was critical of the intense fear of biblical scholarship which pervaded the Roman Catholic Church at that time.

Improved ecumenism in the present climate has led to an atmosphere more cordial than that of 1953. It is also true to say that much of the force of his criticism of Roman Catholic doctrine and practice has been lessened in recent years by a careful redefinition of many of the points to which he raised objections. His obituary in the *Church Times* recorded 'it is likely that he would gladly assert today that there was now less need for such a work'.[5] Other literary activities included book reviews, 'clear, concise and amusing', for the parish paper as well as for the *Church Times* through which he reached a world wide readership. He was their theological adviser from 1961 to 1967, and apart from writing occasional leading articles, ran a regular feature called 'Personal Posers', known in certain quarters as 'Ross-on-Why', in which he dealt with almost any situation which might confront the perplexed Christian. One hundred and nineteen of these were published in his book *Is Religion a Racket?* in 1961. Many of the short, succinct answers that he gave to posed problems are good illustrations of the state of Christian ethics in his day and are by no means outdated.

One of his major concerns was the danger posed by the spread and increasing attractiveness of various deviant and heretical sects and cults such as the Mormons, Jehovah's Witnesses, Christian Science, Astrology, Spiritualism and Seventh Day Adventism. In 1954 and 1956 he published five pamphlets in which he neatly demolished their claimed foundations. In

February 1960, he delivered a series of lectures at the University of Durham on the same subjects, and these were published in 1961 under the title *Dangerous Delusions*. His research into these various cults caused him to draw a number of interesting conclusions, of which the foremost was a common desire for a certainty in faith which God does not choose to give. He also discerned the major role played by women in many of these cults: Mary Baker Eddy in Christian Science; Helena Blavatsky and Annie Besant in Theosophy; and Ellen White in Seventh Day Adventism. He drew the conclusion that Christianity was plainly too masculine and that the modern church was not making the best use of women. He also noted that the success of many of the cults was due to their biblical fundamentalism, and that the mainstream churches had failed to provide people with a proper understanding of the Bible, thereby giving them the means with which to combat the claims of rigid fundamentalism. 'We must come clean and explain what the Bible really is, and expound its main themes, and encourage true Bible Study in homes and groups . . . we must not leave our people unprotected'.[6]

Kenneth Ross's output was prolific (twenty-five separate publications between 1945 and 1974), well-written, easy to read but learned nonetheless. Looking at a list of his publications, there would seem to be little order to their appearance and content – more a series of responses to existing situations. The most famous, with the possible exception of *Why I am not a Roman Catholic*, is his *Letter to a Homosexual*, first published in 1955. It was a compassionate treatment of the subject and showed that he had a depth of understanding far in advance of his time. Many observed that the book represented a new stage in the Church's understanding and attitude towards the subject. Most of his publications were written

157

All Saints' Church, the east end, 1965

during the strenuous years at All Saints', the last
being *What the Spirit says to the Churches*, in 1965.
Thereafter, the growing problem of the Choir School
finances, leading to the announcement in 1967 that it
would close at Easter 1968, and his own departure
from All Saints' in 1969, curtailed any thought of
writing. He had made plans for a book on the practice
of hearing confessions; these were temporarily halted

All Saints' Church, the west end, 1965

by his death in 1970. The manuscript was subsequently prepared for publication by Canon Reginald Cant of York Minster, and it appeared in 1974 under the title *Hearing Confessions*.

It is something of a surprise that he never published anything in the field of liturgy since he was a very accomplished liturgist and spent several years on the Liturgical Commission of the Church of

England. He experimented with the liturgy of All Saints' in minor ways, with strict perimeters. The use of birettas and maniples was discontinued in his time, and a change was made from the Book of Common Prayer to Series 1 in the mid-1960s. By the beginning of that decade, All Saints' was beginning to see a sharp increase in the number of communicants at the High Mass, falling in line with the growing practice of congregational communion at the main Sunday Eucharist. Not all the congregation availed themselves of this at first, much to Ross's relief, and he continued to encourage communion at the earlier masses. An evening mass was established regularly from 1965; though while he recognized that this enabled many more people to make their communion and to observe days of obligation, the worry about inadequate preparation caused him some misgiving.

The period of liturgical reform in the Church of England coincided with a similar period in the Roman Catholic Church, and Ross was cognizant of the fact, though he was never a great Romanist. He was sensitive to and sensible of movements in Roman liturgiology, but there was never any question of slavishly following the path of Rome. In a related area, he never went to Walsingham and had no great regard for the Shrine and its activities. When the proposals for Anglican-Methodist unity were being discussed in the late 1960s, he distanced himself from the mainstream of the Catholic movement in the Church of England by vigorously supporting them, and the failure of the scheme in 1969 came as a severe blow. Although he was a member of the executive of the Church Union, he was a 'liberal' catholic in the best sense of that word.

Like so many of his predecessors, Kenneth Ross was a master of the pulpit. He spent a great deal of time on the preparation of his sermons, and was often weeks ahead in writing them. He was known to be writing his Easter sermons on Boxing Day. He was an undemonstrative preacher who delivered sermons that were full of feeling but were nonetheless quite unexcited – and the congregation always listened. One of his distinctive mannerisms was to drape his hands over the edge of the pulpit as though they were hanging out to dry. His rather chatty style of preaching was 'enlivened by quiet touches of humour which his manner of delivery brought out to perfection. Even in the days when congregations were more inhibited than they are today, there could be ripples of laughter'.[7] He was a great populariser of what he knew. Perhaps because he had read and thought so deeply about what he wanted to say and because he knew his congregation and at what level to pitch his sermon, he was a successful preacher.

His other great gifts lay in the ministries of confession and spiritual direction and he was known to spend long hours in the confessional hearing the confessions of his large number of penitents. 'His unlimited patience, his understanding of the mixtures of motives underlying all our actions, of our boundless capacity for self-deception and of the need to distinguish between sin and temptation . . . were qualities which made him the most sought-after confessor in London. He was never dogmatic, and when asked to advise on a matter about which differing opinions might conscientiously be held, he would point out that a different counsellor would probably give a different answer, always making the enquirer responsible for his own decisions; his aim was the spiritual growth of those who sought his counsel'.[8]

He was hampered to some extent by his shyness which meant that whereas he could speak with clarity and directness from the pulpit and in the confessional, or when reading a well-prepared paper

161

to an audience, he was ill at ease in social company to the point of being stiff and inarticulate. And when he was nervous or had something unpleasant to say, he tended to blink and look sideways. This was an unfortunate image because beneath it all he was a warm, loving and approachable person, though those who sought his help would have to approach him, he would never do the approaching. As one of his curates remarked, 'he kept an iron control of himself'.

His administration of the parish was less successful, as seen in the affair of the closure of the Choir School. For all his liberalism in certain areas, Kenneth Ross was essentially an old-fashioned Anglo-Catholic priest in his administration of the parish. There were no staff meetings, nothing in the way of forward planning, no discussion of what was to happen. He took all the major decisions himself without any thought of consulting who might be affected in any way. One of his curates recalled that with the other curate he visited the Vicar's study on parochial business only twice in five years. He never entertained his curates or parishioners, except for the one occasion on his silver jubilee as a priest in 1957, when he took the curates, the wardens, the organist, his mother and sisters to a restaurant in Duke Street. He could be very funny and very encouraging when he felt it right but he never threw compliments around, and although he only criticised the sermons of others on the rarest of occasions, he could be acidly direct. One visiting preacher chose to preach on the subject of the deep friendship and relationship between David and Jonathan. The preacher went on and on about the wonderful friendship between the two men until finally, Kenneth Ross's legendary patience and sensitivity snapped, and he was heard, sitting in the sanctuary, to mutter, 'Oh God – will nothing stop him!'. A curate was even more unfortunate, in receiving a very cutting remark after the Mass on asking his Vicar whether his sermon had been up to the latter's standard. Ross replied icily 'Most I could not hear, and what I could I regretted'.

The high point of the incumbency of Kenneth Ross was the celebration in 1959 of the centenary of the consecration of the church, an event which rivalled Dom Bernard's celebration of the centenary of Frederick Oakeley's licensing in 1939. The programme was as follows:

Wednesday 27 May

6 pm   Solemn Evensong, Procession and
       Benediction
       Preacher: The Vicar

Thursday 28 May CORPUS CHRISTI

11 am   High Mass
        Preacher: The Reverend Cyril Tomkinson
6 pm   Solemn Evensong and Benediction
       Preacher: The Rt Revd Mark Carpenter-
       Garnier

Friday 29 May CENTENARY OF THE CONSECRATION

11 am   Procession and High Mass
        Preacher: The Bishop of London
6 pm   Solemn Evensong, Te Deum and Benediction
       Preacher: The Reverend Fr F. B. Dalby,
       Superior of SSJE

Saturday 30 May EXTERIOR SOLEMNITY OF CORPUS CHRISTI

11 am   High Mass
        Celebrant: The Bishop of Malmesbury
        Preacher: The Reverend E. L. Mascall

163

2.45   Solemn Procession of the Most Holy
Sacrament
Preacher: The Bishop of Crediton
(The canopy over the Blessed Sacrament was
borne by four Doctors of Divinity)
6 pm Solemn Evensong
Preacher: The Bishop of Malmesbury

Sunday 31 May TRINITY 1

11 am Procession and High Mass of the Dedication
Preacher: The Archbishop of York
6 pm Solemn Evensong, Procession and
Benediction
Preacher: The Abbot of Nashdom

Monday 1 June OF THE DEDICATION

11 am High Mass
Preacher: The Reverend Fr Paul Hume,
Director of SSM
6 pm Solemn Evensong
Preacher: The Reverend Fr Trevor
Huddleston, CR

Tuesday 2 June COMMEMORATION OF DEPARTED PRIESTS, BENEFACTORS AND WORSHIPPERS

11 am High Mass
Celebrant: The Bishop of Kensington
Preacher: The Dean of Lincoln
6 pm Solemn Evensong
Preacher: The Dean of Westminster

Wednesday 3 June OF THE DEDICATION

11 am High Mass
Preacher: The Bishop of Willesden

6 pm   Solemn Evensong
       Preacher: The Reverend Fr Lothian,
       Assistant Minister of the Society of St Francis

Thursday 4 June OF THE DEDICATION

11 am High Mass
       Preacher: The Rt Reverend and Rt Hon
       William Wand, Canon of St Paul's Cathedral
 6 pm Solemn Evensong, Procession and
       Benediction
       Preacher: The Rt Reverend Kenneth
       Mackenzie

The one hundredth birthday of the church was an occasion for much celebration and rejoicing. All Saints' had survived early stern disapproval, countless financial crises, the depopulation of its geographical parish, the demolition and closure of several other churches in the deanery, and many other problems, but it still survived. All Saints', Margaret Street, in 1959, was in a quite different situation from the days of Oakeley and Upton Richards. The parish congregation had effectively ceased to exist and the eclectic congregation had taken over. If the church was to survive, it had to maintain those principles on which it had been built, mainly as a centre of spiritual, musical and liturgical experience. The concept of All Saints' as a parish church was now quite out of date. People visited All Saints' mainly to pray and to worship, but also to watch and to listen – to watch the liturgy and to listen to the music. In the years after the Second World War – which effectively finished the parish as a residential area – the preaching, the liturgy and the music all grew in importance.

All Saints' was now one of the few surviving parish churches left in the country maintaining a resident choir school. The origins of the school went back to 1848 when the first chorister was admitted. It was closed down between 1854 and 1859 because the expense of building the new church excluded the possibility of maintaining the school as well. It is not an exaggeration to say that throughout its 120-year history it maintained a precarious existence, ever plagued by the worries of money and other matters. By 1966, it was clear that the school could not survive in its present form and some major decision needed to be made on its future. The problems were partly financial but this was not new. Shortly before the outbreak of the War, Dom Bernard Clements had warned the congregation that the School would have to close if money was not forthcoming. Money was forthcoming and so the School managed to continue for another thirty years, but there were problems of an educational and staffing nature. There were difficulties in finding suitable staff, given the fact that qualified educationalists were not exactly queueing up to teach seventeen boys in a London street. After careful thought and certainly much agonizing, the Vicar and Churchwardens announced immediately after Christmas 1967 that the School would close at Easter 1968. The decision was a hard one and perhaps a lesser man than Kenneth Ross would have shirked the issue by moving on and leaving his successor to deal with the problem.

The reaction was predictable. Letters poured into the Vicarage, some of them expressing sentiments quite out of keeping with the virtues of love and compassion taught by Christ. Letters went to the *Church Times* accusing the Vicar of being high-handed and authoritarian, arrogant and autocratic and refusing to fight to keep the School open. While not doubting that the closure of the Choir School was a loss to the tradition of All Saints' and also to the rest of the Church, we do feel that, nearly twenty years after the event, the incident does need to be put into some kind of perspective, if only to salvage something of the reputation of Kenneth Ross himself. In her article 'Kenneth Needham Ross: the Margaret Street Years', published in the Spring 1984 edition of *Christian*, Margaret Hodgetts described the School as an educational anachronism. 'Those who were most closely connected with the School had realised that its eventual closure was inevitable, and there had been warnings given by successive headmasters'. She quoted a former churchwarden as saying that the Choir School was 'one of the brightest jewels in the crown of All Saints'. 'Did he [Kenneth Ross] also have a sense of the correct order of priority in the organization of a church? Perhaps the counting of jewels in a crown should not head the list'.[9]

Those who knew Kenneth Ross at the time of the closure recall that he was deeply wounded and hurt by the storm of criticism that greeted his decision. He was an old-fashioned Anglo-Catholic priest who was shocked by the fact that his congregation simply did not trust him to take the right decision. The protests which greeted the closure were probably due more to the way in which he handled the affair than to a misjudgement on his part. He had examined the whole situation, found the problems to be insoluble, consulted his churchwardens and announced his decision. There was no thought of preparing the way by discussion with the organist or curates, or laying the facts of the matter before the Parochial Church Council or congregation and warning them that closure might be necessary. His decision was based entirely on his careful estimate of the situation. But though he anticipated some criticism he failed to foresee its extent and its depth. All his decisions were made that way without any perceived need for consultation with his colleagues. That was the way he had always worked and he was genuinely hurt by

167

public reaction because he saw it as a reflection on his own position as the parish priest, and a criticism of his power of judgement.

To a church where the maintenance of tradition had come to be paramount, the end of the Choir School was greeted with scenes approaching hysteria in certain quarters, but writing twenty years after the event, we find ourselves wondering what all the fuss was about. The musical tradition of the church hardly suffered at all, since, almost immediately, the boys were replaced by sopranos and the repertoire was enlarged.

Unfortunately for Kenneth Ross, his cup of sorrow was still not full. The closure of the Choir School was followed by the rejection in 1969 of the proposed scheme for unity between the Church of England and the Methodist Church. The scheme had his full support, much to the annoyance of clergy of his own tradition who were critical of him for not following the Catholic 'line'. Their chief objection to the scheme lay in the ambiguous wording of the service of reconciliation. Ross replied to these anxieties in a way which demonstrated his strong faith in the efficacy of sacramental grace, a grace which could not be limited by human authority. 'What is certain is that the clearly expressed intention of the service is that, through the laying on of the Bishop's hands, whatever the Methodist minister needs in order to celebrate with full validity of order and jurisdiction may be given to him . . . He may need much, he may need everything: on the other hand, he may need little, he may need nothing. But much or little, all or nothing, whatever he requires, he receives'.[10]

The rejection of the scheme was a grievous blow and he felt that Methodists should not be blamed if they wanted nothing further to do with reunion. 'The value of episcopal government must be rather

Kenneth Ross (centre) with the boys of the Choir School

obscure to them when they see the bishops flouted so
extensively . . . Perhaps God will deal mercifully with
our cowardice and diminish the penalty which we
deserve'.[11]

By 1969, Kenneth Ross had spent eighteen years
as Vicar of the difficult parish of All Saints' and, like
so many of his predecessors, he was tired and
dispirited. His work at All Saints' was outstanding,
but he was never offered preferment when he needed
rest from his labours, though, in fairness to the
authorities, he himself never gave any indication that
he sought or expected preferment. Eventually the
twin blows of the Choir School closure and the failure
of the unity scheme caused him to accept the offer of
the position of Chancellor and Canon Residentiary of
Wells Cathedral in September 1969. He spent nine
months there of complete happiness, dying in a
Bristol hospital on 8 June 1970 after a few days of
acute heart trouble. After cremation, his ashes were
buried in the cloister garden at Wells, and a Mass of
Requiem was sung at All Saints' on 20 June.

Looking back at the life and work of Kenneth Ross, eighth Vicar of All Saints', we have no doubt that he was a man of great holiness, serving God and serving his people with complete devotion to both. His own lifestyle was austere and frugal to the point that he would sooner wrap himself up as best he could and shiver while working, rather than turn on a heater during Lent. At Old Malden he was remembered as fasting so severely during the season that he could barely stand at the altar through weakness. His learning was profound and wide-ranging, and he enjoyed many continental holidays, leaving nothing unseen that was of any cultural interest. Concerts, art galleries and museums provided him with great pleasure, and in his last years he travelled in Greece with his sisters. When he was once asked how he had spent the afternoon of a particular day, he replied, 'Reading five French novels'.

Shy, quiet, gentle and kind, the death of this unassuming priest at the age of only sixty-one was a distressingly early loss to the Church of England.

CHAPTER NINE

THE EVANGELIST
MICHAEL MARSHALL
1969–1975

'It is perhaps in the realm of the doctrine of preaching that the Church in recent decades has lost its nerve most conspicuously, so there can be no doubt that we need to recover our doctrine in this field if we are to recover our confidence as preachers. For supremely, preaching is the activity of God: it is an event and not simply an essay or an exercise'

(Michael Marshall, *Renewal in Worship*, London, 1982, p. 128)

Michael Marshall, 9th Vicar, 1969–1975, at his induction as Vicar of All Saints', with the Venerable H. A. S. Pink, Archdeacon of Hampstead 1964–1974

MICHAEL ERIC MARSHALL

Born: 14 April 1936
Christ's College, Cambridge 1955–1958
Cuddesdon Theological College 1958–1960
Deacon 1960   Priest 1961
Curate of St Peter's, Birmingham 1960–1962
Tutor at Ely Theological College 1962–1964
Honorary Minor Canon of Ely Cathedral 1962–1964
Chaplain, University of London 1964–1969
Vicar of All Saints', Margaret Street 1969–1975
Bishop 1975
Bishop Suffragan of Woolwich 1975–1984
Director of the Anglican Institute 1984–

DESPITE the great spirituality that Kenneth Ross undoubtedly possessed, he was a tired man by the end of the 1960s, and his style of priesthood, reserved and austere as it was, needed to be replaced by something more vigorous in the London of the 1960s. Many felt that the turmoil of that decade required a response from the Church that was fresh and invigorating. Not only was there a need to ensure that the new Vicar of All Saints' was as different from Kenneth Ross as the latter had been from Cyril Tomkinson, to prevent any unfavourable comparisons being made, but that he should be equipped to meet the challenges facing the Church in the midst of social and cultural upheaval.

The division of the Diocese of London into defined geographical areas under the effective episcopal oversight of the Suffragan Bishops of the Diocese meant that All Saints' now fell within the pastoral jurisdiction of the Bishop of Willesden whose area included Westminster. The Bishop of Willesden at that time was the Right Reverend Graham Leonard (Bishop of London since 1981), and the task of choosing a new Vicar for All Saints' fell to him. His choice proved to be a surprise. The ninth Vicar of All Saints' was to be the Reverend Michael Eric Marshall, a thirty-three year old Chaplain to the University of London. He was the youngest incumbent in the history of the Church, his closest rival being William Upton Richards, who was licensed as Minister of the Margaret Chapel in 1845 at the age of thirty-four. Telling the story of his incumbency and his life is not so straightforward as with his eight predecessors, if only for the fact that he is still alive at the time of writing.

Michael Eric Marshall was born on 14 April 1936 into a Roman Catholic Lincolnshire family. He was educated at Lincoln School and at Christ's College, Cambridge, where he took a degree in History and

Theology. Having been received into the Church of England and discerning a vocation to the priesthood, he went to Cuddesdon Theological College for two years, and was ordained Deacon in 1960 and Priest in 1961, serving his title at the inner city parish of St Peter's, Birmingham. He left there in 1962 to take up the posts of Tutor at Ely Theological College and Minor Canon of Ely Cathedral, where he remained until the closure of the College two years later. From Ely he moved to be a chaplain of the University of London, based at the University Church of Christ the King in Gordon Square. After a highly successful pastoral ministry lasting five years, during which time he developed his flair for the imaginative use of all available space in the church premises, or 'plant' as he termed it, he moved to All Saints', Margaret Street in the autumn of 1969.

The interregnum between Kenneth Ross and Michael Marshall was comparatively short, the former leaving at the beginning of September, and the induction of the latter taking place on 29th October. It was a grand occasion, the arrival of the Bishop being greeted by a fanfare sounded by trumpeters of the Life Guards, and then by the singing of the *Ecce Sacerdos Magnus* by Bruckner. Among the visiting dignitaries present in the Choir was the Right Reverend Edward Roberts, Bishop of Ely, who had served as Curate under Henry Mackay and Dom Bernard Clements.

Much of the ministry of Michael Marshall at All Saints' Church was bound up with the phenomenon known as the Institute of Christian Studies which came into formal existence in 1973, though it began its life under a different appearance in 1970. Although it is remembered as the creation of Michael Marshall, its real origins lie with Bishop Leonard. He conceived the idea of All Saints' being used as a catechetical centre or Secular Institute, a place that

175

would produce a theologically well-educated and articulate laity. The closure of the Choir School in 1968 had left Numbers 8 and 84 Margaret Street free for development, and, in one sense, the creation of the Institute filled the vacuum caused by that closure. All Saints' had lost a large portion of its community life with the departure of the boys, and many people felt, wrongly, that the Church had lost its sense of direction. So much energy and money had been channelled into maintaining the Choir School over so many years that its final closure did produce a feeling that All Saints' had no future; that it was nothing without the School. Bishop Leonard's concept of a catechetical centre was a vision needed by All Saints' to give it a sense of purpose and direction. An appeal for £10,000 was launched. Number 84 Margaret Street (across the road from the Church) was used to provide accommodation in the form of bed-sitting rooms, and Number 8, parts of Number 6 and the basement of the Vicarage (Number 7) were used to provide a common room, lecture room and refectory; the old Choir School kitchen became a bar where Institute members and parishioners could meet together. The Bishop had envisaged a residential catechumenate, which took the form of about ten people living at Number 84, and a series of high-powered visiting lecturers who were to lecture to open audiences. As the plan turned out, the Monday lectures were delivered by distinguished visitors, and the Thursday lectures by the resident clergy of All Saints'. All the lectures were open to the public. The resident community at Number 84 provided the 'membership' of the Institute and those who attended the lectures were styled associate members. The members came from varying backgrounds and occupations and included teachers, local shop and social workers.

In this form, the Institute lasted for about three

years. By 1973, a change in its organization and thrust had become necessary with the growing realization that although there were large numbers of people who wished to take advantage of the opportunities of studying presented by the Institute and its courses, not many of them wished to live in, and difficulty was experienced in filling the vacant places at Number 84 with suitable people. Further problems were caused by the cramped accommodation in Number 8. The lectures were very well attended, and were outgrowing the very limited room space in the old Choir School. A decision was taken to abandon the existing residential catechumenate and to continue the Institute solely as a teaching body. Another appeal was launched to transform Number 84 into the headquarters of the Institute and to construct a small chapel in the basement. The new Institute was formally inaugurated by Archbishop Michael Ramsay of Canterbury on All Saints' Day 1973. Lectures and seminars were held on four nights of the week and the Institute had a membership of 200 by 1977. In this new form it ceased to bear much resemblance to what Michael Marshall had established in 1970, but he loyally supported it, spending two evenings a week there. The day-to-day running of the Institute was managed by John Slater (Curate 1970–77) with the title of Principal.

We have felt it worthwhile to record the history of the Institute because it remains so closely identified with the incumbency of Michael Marshall, being in one sense the victim of its own success, as similar 'night schools' were opened in parishes outside central London. Although its life was comparatively brief (it effectively closed in the summer of 1978), it did much to reinvigorate the life of All Saints' after the departure of the Choir School and to give the church, albeit briefly, a new sense of direction.

By virtue of the fact that he was only thirty-three

at the time of his induction, Michael Marshall breathed fresh air into the life of the parish. His youth gave him vigour and the years of his incumbency were nothing if not exciting ones. In the tradition of his predecessors, he had great preaching ability and could illustrate his sermons with image after image. He had a talent for communicating the Christian faith with a flamboyant incisiveness. The same flamboyance extended to the celebration of the liturgy, though here he was much less at ease than in the pulpit. The staid formality of the liturgy at All Saints' caused him a degree of irritation, though he was content to make only minor alterations, and he felt the constraints imposed by such a tradition.

His first book, of which he was the sole author, was *Glory Under Your Feet*, published in 1978 at the time of the movement for Catholic Renewal in the Church of England. He began with a survey of the contemporary religious climate, concluding that there was no prospect of religion disappearing from the world scene, any more than there was of the state withering away in orthodox Marxism. 'Man is a compulsive worshipper and sooner or later his religious instincts will have their say. We ignore the power of religion at our peril as a civilisation. It will not go away; it will become converted or perverted . . . a society or civilisation which supposes that it has grown beyond religion and its needs is always the one most easily duped and most ready to revert to the horrors of primitive religious convictions and behaviour'.[1] Marshall recalled his experiences at a mission to the University of Oxford in 1969 at which he was a joint leader with Bishop Ian Ramsey and Archbishop Anthony Bloom. Ian Ramsey's carefully constructed and brilliant arguments on the rational basis for belief were not well attended, unlike the daily 'School of Prayer' conducted by Archbishop Bloom, in which he totally by-passed intellectual issues and plunged straight into the experiential and the spiritual. 'For me that was a significant moment – it marked the end of the tyranny of the rational and the beginning of the seduction of the spiritual and the charismatic'.[2] He expressed his alarm at the growth of gnosticism in various forms and called for a renewal of catholic Christianity to counter this 'bondage of religious taboos and fears'. He urged a new struggle for renewal in the major areas of catholicity, apostolicity, holiness, the church, and unity.

Further books appeared through the 1980s. *Pilgrimage and Promise* was the Archbishop of Canterbury's Lent Book for 1981 and dealt with the Christian life as a journey and a pilgrimage. *Renewal in Worship* was published in 1982. In the Preface he told of his fear that those people who were returning to Christian life and commitment might find the worship of the Church to be the biggest stumbling-block to living faith. As his reasons, he gave the liturgical revision of the second half of the twentieth century as a lengthy and disturbing process with which few clergy and laity had yet come to terms; many of the clergy who held positions of authority in the church had lived through a time when worship ranked low on the agenda of the church. 'There was a fear and unquestioned assumption in the 'fifties and 'sixties that to be concerned with the details of worship was to turn your back on the more serious and compelling issues of the world and contemporary society'.[3] He described the book as a challenge to all those who were charged with the ministry of the word and sacrament. 'If this is your calling, nothing can be spared in making certain that for those who already come to church a banquet of the word and worship is being prepared for next Sunday or whenever and wherever God's people are next to meet for worship'. Such care would properly equip the people of God for all the other ministries and tasks. 'The renewal of the churches today converges on worship and commitment and then explodes outwards in evangelism, service and concern for the world'.[4] The book dealt, competently and imaginatively, with such diverse ingredients of worship as bread and wine, and the use of candles, water, oil, music, stillness and space. 'All our worship must bring us into the kingdom and raise us into the fellowship of the saints, together with 'angels and archangels and all the whole company of heaven'. Only such heavenly worship is any earthly use at all'.[5] Hearts, heavy with the concerns of the world and the community in which they existed, must be raised, if they were ever to be of any help to that community and raise it into the presence of God through the intercession.

In 1975, after a five-and-a-half year ministry at All Saints', Michael Marshall accepted the offer of Mervyn Stockwood, Bishop of Southwark, to become Bishop Suffragan of Woolwich. It cannot have been an easy choice after such a short period at All Saints' and with so much still to be done, but to Woolwich he went. His departure was announced on Low Sunday (6th April) and he was consecrated in Westminster Abbey on 23 September 1975.

During his time as Bishop of Woolwich he established a reputation for thorough and conscientious parochial visitations. He also attempted to found another residential community on the lines of the original Institute, in the old Rectory of St Mary's, Lewisham. The attempt failed through lack of support. There is some evidence to justify the impression that he was not entirely happy with his role as a suffragan bishop, particularly its administrative demands, and towards the end of his time in the Diocese of Southwark he began to show a restlessness not unlike that of Cyril Tomkinson. He resigned in 1984, amid general surprise, to accept the post of Episcopal Director of the newly-created

Anglican Institute based at a parish in St Louis, Missouri in the United States. The Institute was founded with the task 'to tell and re-tell the Gospel story, to understand the unique and lasting revelation of Jesus as Christ; to rekindle the fire of faith and to re-awaken an appreciation of the riches of the Anglican tradition of worship . . . with outreach to parishes and dioceses of the Episcopal Church of the United States of America, as well as throughout the world-wide Anglican Communion. The primary thrust of the Institute is to foster the teaching of the Gospel of Jesus Christ in an Anglican context'.[6]

Four years after its establishment, we find it difficult, at this distance, to make any assessment of the work of this Institute and the extent to which it has fulfilled the tasks it set itself and the expectations it aroused. Little seems to be heard of it in the United Kingdom, and the inclination is to say that it has made little impact outside the United States. Its future, and the future of its Director, must remain a matter for speculation.

No one can doubt that Michael Marshall is a man of tremendous verbal ability, which he uses to great effect in the medium of the pulpit. His flamboyant and exhortatory style of preaching attracted a considerable following at All Saints', and his great mistake was to leave the church so soon without putting the fledgling Institute of Christian Studies on a stronger financial and administrative base. His very style and personality were, perhaps unconsciously, reflected by the congregation in their perception of the status of All Saints' in the life of the wider church. His consecration to the episcopate at the age of thirty-nine was perhaps too early and could have waited a few more years to allow consolidation of the exciting work done at All Saints' in the years 1969–1975. His resignation of the Bishopric of Woolwich in 1984, though it seemed unwise in the eyes of many at the

181

Michael Marshall (on the right) after his consecration as Bishop of Woolwich on 23 September 1975. With him are Ronald Gordon, Bishop of Portsmouth 1975–1984, and Donald Coggan, Archbishop of Canterbury 1974–1980

time, was probably the right move. Whatever its stated functions, the Anglican Institute, much more so than the Bishopric of Woolwich, provides its Director with a base from which to exercise his considerable talent in an itinerant preaching ministry, a job which he clearly enjoys doing and does very well.

CHAPTER TEN

THE SUFFERER
DAVID SPARROW
1976–1981

'He faced criticism without rancour, disappointment without resentment; he accepted pain without complaint. A man of high principles and strong convictions, his sympathy and understanding widened, his faith and trust grew'

(Bishop Anthony Tremlett writing in the Parish Paper for September 1981)

David Sparrow, 10th Vicar, 1976–1981

DAVID ALAN SPARROW

Born: 22 April 1936
Pembroke College, Oxford 1956–1961
Lincoln Theological College 1961–1962
Deacon 1962   Priest 1963
Curate of St Stephen with St John, Westminster
1962–1966
Chaplain to the Archbishop of Canterbury 1966–1967
Chaplain of St Catherine's College, Cambridge
1967–1976
(Fellow of St Catherine's College 1969–1976)
Vicar of All Saints', Margaret Street 1976–1981
Died: 26 July 1981

AFTER the departure of Michael Marshall on Holy Cross Day (14th September) 1975, the announcement of the name of his successor was awaited with eagerness, the appointment being in the gift of the Right Reverend Gerald Ellison (Bishop of London 1973–1981). Events moved swiftly, and in December of that year the appointment was announced of David Sparrow, Fellow and Chaplain of St Catherine's College, Cambridge, as the tenth Vicar. Following a priest of such high profile, David Sparrow's task was not easy from the beginning, and for much of his brief ministry at All Saints' he laboured under the difficulty of following a popular predecessor. Shortly before his death he preached a moving sermon, which was to be one of his last, and which was in effect his spiritual testament. It was published in the Parish Paper for August 1981 and in it he disclosed something of his early feelings when he said that, as a young priest, he had decided that when the time came for him to accept an incumbency, he would lay down three conditions before accepting any job. Firstly, he would not want the task of following a popular incumbent, with whom he would be constantly compared. Secondly, he had no wish to go to a church in financial difficulty, since he would have to spend most of his time fund-raising. Thirdly, he would prefer a poorly-attended church which would give him a free hand to rebuild a worshipping Christian community with little restraint from the past. It remains a considerable credit to David Sparrow that in accepting All Saints' he followed a popular incumbent, inherited a full church, and had to spend most of his time raising money for the extensive restoration work that needed to be done to the roof and sanctuary walls. It is unlikely that he would have chosen All Saints' for his ministry under such circumstances, and his early death was a great loss for All Saints' and for the wider Church. But he was always conscious of his duty to do the will of God, and to see a sense of purpose wherever he was. 'As God observed this self-regarding meditation, He smiled to Himself and decided to deal with this naughty cleric and, with a gentle sense of irony, He sent me to All Saints', Margaret Street'.[1]

David Sparrow was born in the north London suburb of Finchley on 22 April 1936, and as a boy sang in the choir of St Luke's Church, Mountfield Road, where he was later confirmed. He went to Finchley Grammar School, and then did National Service in the Royal Air Force. On his release he went to Pembroke College, Oxford where he spent five years reading History and Theology. On graduating in 1961, he spent a year at Lincoln Theological College (Cuddesdon having been his first choice) and was ordained deacon in 1962. He served his title at the parish of St Stephen, Rochester Row, in Westminster. St Stephen's was a large and flourishing parish with the now unheard-of status of having seven curates, and a recently-completed daughter church dedicated to St John the Evangelist in Causton Street (now London Diocesan House). He was later given joint charge of St John's and built up a congregation of more than a hundred communicants from the surrounding Peabody Estate.

In 1966 he moved across the Thames to become Domestic Chaplain to the Archbishop of Canterbury, then Michael Ramsay. As the junior of the two Chaplains he was largely responsible for the Lambeth Palace end of the day-to-day business of the Diocese of Canterbury, and spent most weekends with the Archbishop in the Old Palace at Canterbury, visiting the clergy and parishes of Kent. He was also concerned with diocesan ordinands, a job which gave him much pleasure. He appears to have enjoyed much of the Lambeth work, but found the lack of purely pastoral work somewhat frustrating, and was heard to remark in later years that he spent most of his time ironing the Archbishop's cope. In the following year he was offered the Chaplaincy of St Catherine's College, Cambridge, and felt it right to accept.

Looking back on his ministry, it seems that his time at Cambridge was the happiest period of his life. He was an immediate success at the College, establishing a close relationship with the Master and other members of the Governing Body. He was also on equally easy terms with the undergraduates and the domestic staff and, on one occasion, threw a party for the latter in his rooms. He established a mid-week Eucharist, which drew an attendance of more than forty undergraduates, all of whom he knew by name. After two years he was elected a Fellow of the College and, in 1970, the Bishop of Rochester appointed him to be one of his Examining Chaplains. During university vacations he conducted Ordination and other retreats and was in demand as a visiting preacher. After his death, his former Vicar at St Stephen's, Rochester Row, wrote, 'He was first and foremost a College Chaplain and tried to make the chapel the centre and heart of the community . . . Approachable and friendly by nature, he was easy to get to know. He was very hospitable. His rooms were therefore very seldom empty! With a great sense of humour, and quite unshockable, he was the friend, confidant and adviser to generation after generation of undergraduates – of all sorts and kinds, of all denominations, of all faiths or of none. Without ever being pious, they nevertheless sensed his spirituality, devotion and personal self-discipline and appreciated it and felt better for having known him'.[2] Many of his former students visited All Saints' from time to time. Such a ministry could only be sustained for a limited period and in 1976 he was appointed to succeed Michael Marshall as Vicar of All Saints'. Although he clearly enjoyed his work at Cambridge and missed the sense of fun present in a university environment, he never showed, during his time at All Saints', any regret at having left, saying with typical modesty that he felt he had done enough there and that towards the end he had found the task of learning the names of a new intake of undergraduates each year increasingly difficult.

Though the formal interregnum between the departure of Michael Marshall and the arrival of David Sparrow lasted several months, the announcement of his appointment was not long delayed. The news was widespread by the end of November 1975. He was introduced to the Parochial Church Council on December 10 and preached on the morning of Sunday December 21. The induction was delayed until June 1976 for the obvious and sensible reason of staying at Cambridge until the end of the academic year. He expressed his hopes for the future in the Parish Paper for January 1976. 'It will be a privilege to share in a Christian community where God is so evidently the centre of its existence and the power of its life and where the insights of the Catholic approach are experienced and vindicated in that experience . . . I hope that I shall come to learn from what God has already given and taught you at All Saints' and, with you, be open to His leading and ready to move in obedience into His future for us . . . I come, confident that God has an ongoing purpose and ministry for us all, and I look forward with anticipation and some excitement to discovering the living reality of God's vocation to us'.

David Sparrow's hopes for the future of All Saints' were to take an unexpected turn. Any ideas that he might have had about the future development of the church and his own ministry were thrown off course by the twin blows of the dangerous state of the chancel roof, and the decline in his own health.

189

At the beginning of January 1976, a crack was noticed in the vaulting above the north side of the Choir. The stalls were removed and scaffolding erected to enable a proper inspection to be made. The inspection revealed signs of movement in the chancel vaulting and further monitoring was needed to determine what kind of restoration should be undertaken. In the meantime, the Choir and Sanctuary were not to be used, celebrations taking place instead at a nave altar, with the choir singing in the north aisle. An editorial in the March Parish Paper reported that 'There is every reason to hope that we shall have the choir and sanctuary back in use by Palm Sunday'. The hope proved to be forlorn, and further scaffolding was erected in the chancel, though in such a way as to allow the use of the high altar. By the date of David Sparrow's induction, Friday 18 June at 6.30 in the evening, it had become clear that the church was facing the prospect of having to appeal for £100,000 to pay for major restoration work. As if to underline the problem, a number of tiles on the north wall of the church cracked with a loud noise during the induction. By the autumn, the target had risen to £150,000.

The Induction in comparison to that for Michael Marshall was staid and low key as the Bishop of London, Gerald Ellison, did not consider it appropriate that it should take place in the context of a mass.

The whole question of the restoration of the church, which was to occupy so much of David Sparrow's incumbency, inevitably overshadowed his other work. Given his successful and informal work among undergraduates at St Catherine's, it seemed at times that he felt the constraints imposed by the formality of the liturgy of All Saints'. This was complicated by an attraction to Pentecostalism which he had discovered at Cambridge. One of his first moves was to establish a prayer group, beginning on 7 September, which was to meet in the Vicarage on Tuesday evenings from 8 to 10 pm. It lasted throughout his ministry at All Saints' and for a short while afterwards, and it gave him the kind of informal and intimate spiritual support that only a small group can give, and provided a valuable resource for his spirituality.

The life and worship of All Saints' was not altogether to his liking after the rough and tumble of college life, and he felt that there was a good deal about the worship and spirituality of All Saints' that was superficial. The prayer group was one way in which he tried to remedy this defect. In the Parish Paper for September 1976, he announced an open meeting of all parishioners to be held later that month. It was the first of a number of open meetings which he intended to complement the work of the Annual Meeting to instil a greater sense of unity of mind and purpose among a widely scattered congregation, most of whom knew little of each other. In the Parish paper for January 1979 he wrote, 'As well as the splendid and the public, we need the complementary notes of the intimate and the personal. Our Sunday community needs to be strengthened by the focussing of that common life in smaller groups during the week. Thus the Sunday community will be strengthened by the deepening of the bonds among us and the smaller groups will be saved from being centred on themselves as we all share in the wider grouping . . . In the worship of the small group, there is room for more flexibility and participation . . . Things may properly be more relaxed and free . . . At our parish meeting in September 1976 some spoke of their desire to set up such groups. Now that our church is restored and we can think of other things, I hope that in 1979 we shall be able to get on with it'.

He had an extensive personal pastoral ministry and, like so many priests who are accomplished at spiritual direction or counselling or simply giving advice, he attracted a number of the unstable and insecure, but he never failed to give them time and did his best to cope with their problems.

Though he faithfully maintained the liturgical arrangements at All Saints' roughly as he found them on his arrival, his distinctive spirituality experienced a sense of restriction at having to maintain its formality. As vicar of a non-residential parish, he was not given much chance of pastoral contact with the members of the congregation, a gap only partially filled by the various groups he established. There was a aura of unapproachable reserve about him, as there was with most of his predecessors. If he had a weakness, it was that he internalized his conflicts and could appear to be uptight for much of the time. Again, like previous incumbents, he felt that All Saints' congregation had an exaggerated opinion of itself which needed adjustment from time to time. He was a gifted man, physically impressive in stature, with a deep booming voice, an infectious laugh and a twinkle in his eyes, elegant and incisive in his writing and speech. It was his misfortune to be Vicar of All Saints' at precisely the time when so many of the talents that he had to offer had to be set aside in favour of more mundane efforts such as fund-raising. There was so much that he could have contributed to All Saints', had matters been other than they were.

Only a year or thereabouts after his induction, David Sparrow developed cancer, which clouded the remainder of his incumbency and which ultimately proved fatal. Early in 1979 he went on a seven-week sailing cruise to the Gulf of Mexico, to enable him to convalesce after surgical treatment. After a period of remission, in the summer of 1980, he developed secondaries which by the spring of 1981 had spread

David Sparrow with Cardinal Basil Hume, Archbishop of
Westminster.

widely throughout the body. He was afraid of the
disease, though whether he was afraid of dying is less
easy to discern, and he accepted the diagnosis
unwillingly, knowing all the time that his death might
be necessary. But he was immensely brave and made
no secret of talking about his illness, sometimes from
the pulpit, to the discomfort of a congregation unused
to such open directness, though this was only an
illustration of the way he tackled problems – head on.

It has been suggested that David Sparrow's
greatest contribution to All Saints' was the
tremendous example of the suffering he endured.
Bishop Anthony Tremlett, Vicar of St Stephen's,
Rochester Row, at the time of his curacy there, put it

well in the Parish Paper for September 1981. 'From then onwards he seemed to gain an added dimension. He faced criticism without rancour, disappointment without resentment; he accepted pain without complaint. A man of high principles and strong convictions, his sympathy and understanding widened, his faith and trust grew. His whole ministry reached its climax in the suffering he endured with such courage, and something of its spirit was communicated to the congregation'. During the last few months of his life, when he was no longer able to sing the High Mass on Sundays, his impressiveness grew. Stooped, thin and clearly in considerable pain, he was forced to preach sitting in a chair at the top of the chancel steps. Yet his words rang with deep conviction, and his eyes, though weary with suffering, somehow shone with the brightness of one who had glimpsed something of the eternal glory of the kingdom that awaited him. His voice had lost a little of its power and force, but it became softer and more patient and gentle, as though he understood the words of the hymn by J.M.Neale:

> The trials that beset you,
> The sorrows ye endure,
> The manifold temptations
> That death alone can cure.
>
> What are they but his jewels
> Of right celestial worth?
> What are they but the ladder
> Set up to heaven on earth?

During the last weeks of his life he was confined to his rooms in the Vicarage, as the effects of his illness became more marked. He spent a week in hospital but was able to return home on Saturday 25

July to be with his sister and close friends, and was looking forward to watching the wedding of the Prince of Wales to Lady Diana Spencer on the 29 July. The next morning his condition deteriorated rapidly, but he was able to make his Communion after the High Mass. He died early that afternoon as he had wished, in his home and surrounded by his family and friends, having received the last rites. On the following morning a Low Mass of Requiem was said for the repose of his soul, at 7.30 am. During his entire illness he was nursed with great devotion by Mrs Aileen Buxton, the Sacristan, who, less than a year later, herself died of recurrent cancer.

His remains were received back into All Saints' after Benediction on Sunday 2 August, as the Choir sang the anthem 'Bring us, O Lord God, at our last awakening', by William Harris. Vespers of the Dead was then recited and the coffin remained in church overnight. A Low Mass of Requiem was said the following morning at 9.30 am. It was David Sparrow's express request that the funeral service should take place at St Luke's, Finchley (closed for public worship on 22 February 1981 and demolished in 1986), the church at which he had been a choirboy some forty years earlier. The funeral and the committal at St Marylebone Crematorium were taken by the Archdeacon of London. The memorial service was held at All Saints' Church on Friday 21 August at 6.30 pm. As he had wished, it was entitled a 'Thanksgiving Mass for the Release of the Spirit'. White vestments were worn and the whole service, attended by about 400 friends representing all phases of his life and ministry, was a very happy and moving occasion. The celebrant was Bishop Anthony Tremlett, and the preacher Fr Edwin Barnes, a college contemporary and Vicar of Hessle in Yorkshire. The Deacon of the Mass was Fr James Naters, SSJE, who had acted as confessor to David

Sparrow during his last illness. The collection, for Cancer Relief, amounted to some £500.

Looking back on the life of David Sparrow, we find a slight parallel with George Frederick Holden who also died at an early age before he had a chance to use his considerable talents in the service of the church. Both men went to Pembroke College, Oxford. George Holden laboured throughout his ministry at All Saints' under the sad weight of bereavement, David Sparrow under the weight of cancer. George Holden was Vicar for just under three years and David Sparrow's incumbency lasted for just over five years. So much of what he could have given was suppressed, and so much of what he did give was obliterated, by the problems of finance which have afflicted All Saints' since before it was built. But it would be wrong to say that he died without making his mark. A close friend who visited the church after his arrival, and again shortly before his death, was struck by the change in atmosphere. From being an upstage church and congregation with an acute sense of its own importance, he discerned a change to a much kinder and friendlier atmosphere. If it is true to say that David Sparrow changed under the influence of All Saints', then it is equally true to say that All Saints' changed under the influence of David Sparrow. His suffering and death wrought a change of mentality that was sorely needed and essential for the future life and growth of All Saints'. As he wrote so eloquently in the Parish Paper for July 1977: 'No doctrine, no explication of doctrine . . . will carry authority unless it is validated by the quality of the men and women who profess it, unless it is seen to be the truth as lived. Perhaps Catholics will be heard more when their commitment to the world and its life in concern to express God's caring in meeting suffering and need . . . is more apparent . . . Before we can communicate a living truth, it must have possessed us and become the force in our lives. What we proclaim and who we are must embody a truth of God which meets the actual needs of men, satisfies their hunger, and gives them hope. Then we shall have an authority which will command attention when we speak , . . The most sure and certain way to prepare for revival is to live the truth we profess with greater dedication so that it may be seen in us, however inadequately, that we at least believe it, that it has authority over us and that it is of God, and brings us life.

David Hope, 11th Vicar, 1982–1985

CHAPTER ELEVEN

THE LITURGIST
DAVID HOPE
1982–1985

'In spite of the complexity of the subject,
it is imperative in these days that,
so far as is possible, the evolution and
development of the Christian liturgy
be appreciated and understood by the
individual believer; for ultimately the
liturgy is the means by which, and the
framework within which, the Christian
lives out his day-to-day existence'

(David Hope, *The Leonine Sacramentary*, Oxford,
1970, p. v)

DAVID MICHAEL HOPE

Born: 14 April 1940

University of Nottingham 1959–1962

St Stephen's House and Linacre College, Oxford 1962–1965

Deacon 1965   Priest 1966

Curate of St John The Baptist, Tue Brook 1965–1967 and 1968–1970

Chaplain of the Church of the Resurrection, Bucharest 1967–1968

Vicar of St Andrew's, Oxford 1970–1974

Principal of St Stephen's House, Oxford 1974–1982

Vicar of All Saints', Margaret Street 1982–1985

Bishop 1985

Bishop of Wakefield 1985–

WITH the death of David Sparrow, All Saints' entered an interregnum that was to last for nearly a year. He died in July 1981, and his successor was not instituted until May 1982. It seemed a long time in the eyes of many at the time, though with hindsight, and whether done intentionally or unintentionally, it was a wise course. Fr Sparrow had been incapacitated by cancer, to a greater or lesser degree, throughout most of his incumbency, and towards the end, the experience of watching their parish priest die was something of an emotional strain on the congregation. The gap of ten months was needed to enable the strain to ease and to allow feelings of bereavement to run their full course.

As patron of the benefice, the Bishop of London (since early 1981, the Right Reverend Graham Leonard, who had been responsible for the appointment of Michael Marshall in 1969 and the setting up of the Institute of Christian Studies) had the duty of appointing the new Vicar. The Parochial Church Council was entitled to make known to the Bishop its views on the needs of the parish and the qualities it sought in a new Vicar – but without mentioning names. The Council, attended by the Archdeacon of London, met on 4 August and then adjourned until September to prepare its brief on the needs of the parish for submisson to the Bishop. Consultation between the Bishop and the Churchwardens took place in the autumn, and on 25 November, the name of the new Vicar was publicly announced. Rumours had begun to leak out for some weeks previously before the announcement that the Reverend David Michael Hope, Principal of St Stephen's House, Oxford, was to be the new Vicar.

David Hope was born on 14 April 1940 at Wakefield in Yorkshire where, as a boy, he sang in the choir of the Cathedral Church of All Saints. He graduated from the University of Nottingham in 1962

201

going to St Stephen's House to study for the priesthood. While at Oxford, he was attached to Linacre College where he undertook research for a thesis on the development of the Western Liturgy in the early Middle Ages under the supervision of Dr F. L. Crosse, Lady Margaret Professor of Divinity in the University. He was awarded the degree of Doctor of Philosophy in 1965 and this thesis was published in 1971 by Oxford University Press under the title *The Leonine Sacramentary*. After ordination in 1965 he served his title at St John the Baptist, Tue Brook, in Liverpool, a well-established centre of Catholicism in the north-west of England. The church had something of a gathered congregation though retained strong parish links. He remained there until 1970 with the exception of a year's leave of absence in 1967–1968 as Chaplain of the only Anglican Church in eastern Europe, the Church of the Resurrection in Bucharest. From there he travelled extensively having been licenced by the Bishop of Gibraltar to minister to the congregations of Anglicans in Yugoslavia and Bulgaria.

In 1970 he was appointed Vicar of St Andrew's, Orford, in Warrington, a town equi-distant between Manchester and Liverpool. It was a new church and parish comprising a housing estate of 18,000–20,000 people with a large infant/junior school. In addition to being Vicar of the parish, he served as a hospital chaplain, was Chaplain to the Mayor of Warrington for one year, and served on the town's education committee.

In 1974, he was persuaded, rumour had it with considerable reluctance, to accept the post of Principal of St Stephen's House, Oxford. Founded in 1876, St Stephen's had long enjoyed the reputation of being the most Catholic of the theological colleges. As such it had been a continuous thorn in the side of the hierarchy of a Church of England never at ease

202

with its Catholic wing despite the work of the Oxford Movement. Viewed with disfavour, few of its students ever found themselves promoted beyond the level of parish priest, and some never got that far. Its consistent and continuous assertion of the principles of the Oxford Movement, combined with its distinctively 'seminary' atmosphere and style of training, ensured that for the greater part of its history it stayed on the periphery of the church, and many of the Bishops were known to look with suspicion at those among their ordination candidates who expressed a desire to be trained at St Stephen's House. This atmosphere and attitude inevitably led to a form of prickly defensiveness on the part of the House and its students, and a 'hothouse' environment developed, partly from this sense of isolated peculiarity, and partly from the unique and proper emphasis on spirituality and priestly formation.

David Hope was appointed Principal of St Stephen's at a time of considerable internal difficulty occasioned by problems of discipline. It was also a time when a number of theological colleges were being closed, and even the concept of residential training itself was being radically questioned. There is no doubt that his eight arduous years as Principal ensured the future of St Stephen's House at a time when there were many calls for its closure. Perhaps his greatest contribution to securing the future of the college was the formidable task of moving it in the summer of 1980 from its existing cramped and unattractive accommodation in Norham Gardens, north Oxford, to the former premises of the Society of St John the Evangelist (the Cowley Fathers) at Marston Street in east Oxford. The move gave St Stephen's House room for expansion within the setting of a complex of monastic buildings set between Iffley and Cowley Roads.

During his time at Oxford, David Hope acquired

a number of distinguished extra-mural appointments. He became a member of the Church of England's Liturgical Commission, playing a significant role in producing new authorized rites for the Liturgies of Holy Week. He was a member of the Finance and Grants Committee of the Advisory Council for the Church's Ministry, and was elected Warden of the Community of St Mary the Virgin at Wantage, one of the largest of the Anglican religious communities. He was also an examining Chaplain to the Bishops of Bath and Wells, Wakefield and Norwich.

The news of his appointment as Vicar of All Saints', Margaret Street in the autumn of 1981 was greeted with great pleasure by the congregation of the church and the students of St Stephen's House, though the latter viewed his impending departure with a certain amount of sadness. There was some expression of surprise at his decision to accept the appointment since he had been heard, on several occasions, to declare his dislike of London and its environment, and his determination not to work there, a declaration which no one seriously believed. David Hope had the reputation of protesting loudly against the thought or possiblity of doing that which he was quite interested in doing. His attitude at the time was sufficient indication that he was pleased to be offered the parish and looked forward to working there. The Churchwardens, Denzil Freeth and Christopher Rawll, were equally pleased and, in a public letter to the congregation issued on 24 November 1981, they declared themselves to be 'at one with the Bishop in believing (him) to be the right man, sent by God to be our Vicar. We commend him to you as an experienced Pastor, a priest with vision holding the full Catholic Faith, a liturgical scholar and a warm and straight-forward Yorkshireman'.

Because of his prior commitments to St

Stephen's House and its students, his arrival at All Saints' was delayed until the end of May 1982. It was a poor choice of timing and subsequent events at St Stephen's proved that it would better have been delayed until the end of the summer term. There seemed to be no obvious choice for this date other than that All Saints' would by then have experienced an interregnum of more than ten months, and some felt that this was long enough.

The institution and induction, in the context of High Mass, was set for Thursday 27 May and was performed by Graham Leonard, Bishop of London, and Frank Harvey, Archdeacon of London, in the presence of the Lord Mayor and Lady Mayoress of Westminster. The occasion was also graced by the presence of four other bishops: Michael Marshall, Edward Roberts, Ambrose Weekes, Suffragan Bishop of Europe and Brian Masters, Bishop of Fulham. Given the small size of the church, the considerable demand for seating, and the necessity of providing seats for official guests, admission to the service had to be by ticket. It was an occasion that combined splendour with the warmth and enthusiasm of welcome. At the time much was made of the fact that the new Vicar's first Sunday in the parish would be Pentecost, the feast day of the Holy Spirit, and there was some speculation, based on casually dropped hints by David Hope, that he would use the occasion to announce changes in the direction of All Saints' and its ministry. In the event, nothing happened.

Within a short time of his arrival, the new Vicar showed that he intended to grasp and, as far as it will ever be possible, solve, the age old problem of church finances. 'All Saints' is famous for its liturgical and musical tradition, but the plain fact of the matter is that our present yearly expenditure substantially outweighs our income and that we cannot allow this state of affairs to continue otherwise we simply pile up an impossible bank overdraft the long term effects of which are horrible to contemplate. The very maintaining of what already we have and appreciate and do is not possible on present financial returns. Hence the need to examine very carefully our needs and resources. It could be a daunting and dispiriting prospect, but we have a very great deal to encourage us, not least the tremendous and magnificent response to the recent All Saint's Festival Appeal. Your readiness and willingness to give so generously in order to try and get rid of the dismal burden of an already heavy bank overdraft before embarking on any Stewardship Renewal programme, this surely ought to give us much confidence and hope for what we are about to embark on in the first quarter of the new year'.[1] And he reiterated the point at the beginning of 1983. 'I make no apology for saying that the first objective is and must be financial: we need more money to be able to do what presently we are doing, and if we are hoping to expand our work from this base, then we shall need the financial resources with which to achieve our aims and objectives'.[2]

On 20 November 1982, he called a Study Conference which assembled in the lecture hall of 84 Margaret Street. Attended by fifty-four members of the congregation, it began with an address by the Vicar on the nature of the church as the people of God. The meeting subsequently divided into six groups for an hour's discussion before reporting back to the whole conference. Broadly the groups felt that two major areas in the life of All Saints' needed improvement, the ministry of welcome and the ministry of teaching. Throughout David Hope's incumbency, much was done to implement these recommendations. The Church began to adopt an atmosphere that was less frigid and exclusive, unfortunate traits that had re-emerged during the interregnum, and more welcoming to new and casual visitors. He emphasised the importance of welcome as an adjunct to mission. 'It was very clear from the Study Day that the whole business of "welcoming" people was a matter for comment, about the ways in which we need to be aware of each other, of the many visitors we are glad to receive, of ensuring that in the words of St Paul we do "welcome one another – as Christ has welcomed you, for the Glory of God". Taking all this a stage further, each of us need only encourage one other person to come with us to All Saints' on a Sunday morning – and we should hardly have enough room for everyone. Yes, we have that basic evangelical pattern of the early apostolic community but have we the same boldness and zeal to bring Christ to others and bring others to him in the fellowship of his body, the Church? Could not one of our new year resolutions be just that – to invite and encourage one other person along with us?'[3]

Lent 1983 was marked down for a Stewardship Renewal Campaign. Only one in a long series designed to clear bank overdrafts and raise the annual income in an attempt to make All Saints' solvent. 'It is essential that we set our finance right and the trend which has persisted for so long, of expenditure substantially outweighing income, be now reversed. Unless we can reach the budget target which we have set ourselves for this coming year and the forecast for the ensuing three years, then we shall seriously have to consider where substantial cuts can be made'.[4]

The word 'cuts' had an ominous ring about it for a church accustomed to a very high and very expensive standard of liturgy and music, and it was difficult to see what cuts could be made without a major change in the character of the liturgy. But, to his credit, David Hope insisted that he would not, under any circumstances, preside over a church sinking deeper and deeper into debt, and cuts would

207

be made where they could achieve a significant reduction in the annual budget. As matters turned out no cuts were necessary at that stage since the Campaign achieved an additional income of £16,000.

Lent 1983 also saw the introduction of a weekday lunchtime mass at 1 pm. It was a sensible innovation which was made permanent at the end of Lent because of its popularity. The church stands in the middle of a district, densely populated with offices and fashion wholesalers in the years since the War, and the previous neglect of this significant period of the day as an opportunity for pastoral affinity for the neighbourhood for the surrounding parish is inexplicable. A further liturgical innovation was made in Holy Week of that year with the introduction of the rarely performed office of Tenebrae on Wednesday evening. Attended by a congregation curious to witness this unusual devotional act, it proved to be a moving prelude to the celebration of the Triduum, and remains an established feature of Holy Week.

The great event of 1983 was the celebration of the 150th anniversary of the Oxford Movement, a gathering force in the life of the Church of England since 1833 when John Keble's Assize Sermon at the Church of St Mary the Virgin in Oxford had begun a movement to recall the Church of England to its Catholic past and its unheeded Catholic provisions. The movement began to achieve toleration, if not respectability, from the latter part of the nineteenth century, and the celebrations of 1983 were accorded official recognition by the presence of the Archbishop of Canterbury at a number of events.

The history of All Saints' Church, beginning with the work of Frederick Oakeley in 1839, made a local celebration inevitable, and it was decided that the anniversary of Keble's Assize Sermon (Sunday 14 July 1833) should be kept on 17 July. Peter Ball,

Bishop of Lewes, preached at the High Mass in the morning, and Bishop Michael Ramsey (Archbishop of Canterbury 1961–1974) preached at Solemn Evensong and Benediction. It was a memorable day which drew large numbers and, for the first time in many years, there was a queue for admission.

As a liturgical scholar, the Rites in use for the weekday and Sunday Masses came under the scrutiny of the new Vicar. At weekday Masses, the old form of Series II (in the morning) and Series III (in the evening) were used, both illegally, since the publication of the Alternative Service Book in 1980. Swift action was needed to restore some kind of order to this chaotic situation. A new arrangement was adopted from September 1982 which fell within the permitted boundaries of the new prayer book. The early morning Mass (and subsequently the lunch time Mass) were said using Rite B from the new book, and the evening Mass was said using Rite A.

Eventually the difficult question of the High Mass had to be tackled. The Vicar outlined the problems in the summer of 1983. 'There are a number of problems here – there are not enough copies of the Service, what copies there are differ at various important points from what we presently do and say, but what we presently do and say is very much of our own order and does not in fact conform to any authorized service for use in the Church of England'.[5] Following discussion and consultation, the Parochial Council decided to adopt Rite B from the new Prayer Book. The Council also decided to adopt the Calendar and Rules to Order the Service from the Book, all from Advent Sunday 1983.

There were a number of less popular innovations, notably the reintroduction of the celebration of the feast of the Assumption of the Blessed Virgin Mary (on 15 August) with a High Mass as a Major Feast in 1983. More controversial was the introduction of the Roman Catholic form of the Divine Praises at Benediction with their references to the Immaculate Conception and Assumption of the Blessed Virgin Mary, doctrines not held by the Church of England. But the introduction of a monstrance at Benediction instead of a covered ciborium, was a welcome improvement.

The celebrations of Holy Week were revised in anticipation of the publication of the now authorized and widely accepted provisions of the Church of England. The major changes were the encouragement of a general communion on Good Friday, the introduction of Tenebrae on the Wednesday of Holy Week, and the restoration of the Vigil element on Holy Saturday night in anticipation of the lighting of the Paschal Candle. The archaic practice of the celebrant alone receiving from the Reserved Sacrament on Good Friday was abandoned and this was generally well-received, though some members of the congregation continued to adhere to the old practice.

Since his days as Principal of St Stephen's House, David Hope had been tipped for high office by those who dabbled in church politics. On more than one occasion his name was linked with a vacant bishopric, though he himself was heard to say that the only office he desired was that of Dean of York Minster. His years in the 'frontline' posts of Principal at St Stephen's and Vicar of All Saints' ensured that he came to the attention of those concerned with filling vacancies at the higher levels, having spent eleven years in these two very public appointments. When he went to All Saints', few, including the churchwardens, expected him to stay for more than a token period before the seemingly inevitable appointment to a bishopric.

Unfortunately for All Saints', the inevitable came sooner than they had expected or hoped. In the early months of 1985, the translation was announced of Colin James, Bishop of Wakefield to the See of Winchester. Almost immediately rumours were started by a number of those who delight in church gossip that David Hope would be his successor. Born in Wakefield, a choir boy at the Cathedral Church, and with his mother, then in her late seventies, living only a few minutes walk away from Bishop's Lodge, David Hope was a natural choice to be the next Bishop. The long expected announcement was made on Tuesday 2 July 1985 to a general mixture of pleasure and dismay at All Saints'. Pleasure that a deserved and long-predicted promotion had come, and dismay that it had come so soon. The consecration took place on Friday 18 October at York Minster, the sermon being preached by Graham Leonard, Bishop of London.

David Hope's incumbency is too recent a period for any objective assessment, and in view of the fact that he is still with us at the time of writing, any estimate of his life and work might be deemed premature. There are one or two parallels with Michael Marshall which could usefully be made. Both stayed at All Saints' for too short a period, and both were preferred to bishoprics at early ages. In the case of David Hope, his brief tenure of the living saw some major accomplishments in the areas of finance and liturgy, but left much still to be done. Towards the end of his time in Margaret Street, his attention was turned towards the dormant Institute of Christian Studies, founded by Michael Marshall in 1970, which has fallen into desuetude in 1978. He began a series of negotiations with the Trustees of the Institute building at 84 Margaret Street, and gave some thoughts to its future and to the appointment of a Principal, but these had reached only preliminary stages before his departure.

Although his promotion seemed to be inevitable,

it came too soon for those at All Saints' who derived considerable benefit from his ministry, and those who hoped that the parish might be on the threshold of some kind of revival. Into its difficult and sometimes prickly atmosphere, he brought a much needed change of air and emphasis. It might be said that his greatest contribution was to turn down the central heating and open the windows, but this would be simplification of the complexity of his character and his abiity which were brought to bear on the life of All Saints'.

Perhaps his greatest strength, and the one from which all his abilities flowed, was the fact that he came from Yorkshire, and never lost his love for that county, always retaining his distinct, though cultured accent. At the time of his death, it was said of William Upton Richards that he had an unaffected simplicity, and that he never adopted the cosmopolitan and diplomatic air usually assumed by clergy seduced by the sophisticated atmosphere of the capital city. The comment equally well applies to David Hope. Though he clearly enjoyed living and working in London and all the benefits that it brought, he never seemed to lose sight of his Yorkshire roots and wisely escaped as often as he could to there and to other parts of the English and Scottish countryside for much needed rest and relaxation. The social whirl of London never affected his lifestyle and outlook in the way that it did for so many other clergy.

Somehow his accent and background seemed to provide a solid assurance that here was no sham facade or display put on to impress or deceive, but a genuine interest in those who talked to him, and concern for their well-being. He had an almost hypnotic ability to calm the nervous, the insecure and the afraid, and persuade them, often for the first time, to articulate their problems and fears. He was a great enabler in the best sense of that word, encouraging

David Hope with Graham Leonard, Bishop of London, at his induction as Vicar of All Saints'

people to think for themselves and to face up to their responsibilities and make their own decisions. He had an impish sense of humour which he used to great effect, partly in helping people to laugh at themselves and partly to entertain, but it was never used destructively, and those who found themselves the butt of his humour generally felt a good deal better for it afterwards.

His powers of intuition and perception were used to great effect and he had a way of getting people to tell him far more than they had intended, not by fierce interrogation but by expressing a gentle interest and concern which was so disarming that he quickly gained the confidence and trust of those who met him. Those who went to him with some private grief or agony found that they were never scolded, but somehow lifted up and sustained by a compassionate regard for their well being.

For all that, he did not suffer fools gladly, and he could react with irritation and impatience when others engaged him at great length on matters that he deemed trifling or inconsequential. It was known that he found the mechanical formality of the liturgy at All Saints' with its emphasis on detail and precision something of a burden, though he was willing to be carried along with it. Had he stayed at the parish for longer than he did, radical changes might have been seen. He could be short-tempered over the pettiness of church politics and gossip, though he was adept at the first and well-informed on the second. He could come to a decision after measured deliberation, but he could also make decisions based on impetuosity. He was often obstinate and difficult to deal with, generally only on substantial matters that he felt were worth fighting for, but occasionally on matters that were small and unimportant. Some of those who came into contact with him found that he could be impossible to deal with, infuriatingly evasive in his answers and in his refusal to be tied down on particular matters. He had the ability to keep his own counsel, and many found to their surprise that the outward (apparently innocent) Yorkshire charm concealed an inner strength of will that they could not manipulate.

His reputation as a man of prayer was considerable, and those who remembered him at St Stephen's House, recalled the hour or more spent in prayer in the College Chapel before the beginning of

Morning Prayer at 7.20 am. This continued at All Saints', to the horror of some, when Morning Prayer on weekdays was moved from 9 am to 6.45 am and followed by a period of silent meditation before the first Mass of the day at 7.30 am. There was an element of the contemplative within him, and he was heard to say that the happiest times were those when he managed to escape for a few days to be alone in some wild and remote part of Scotland, spending his time in silence and stillness away from the many demands made on his time. His chief fault was an inability to say 'no' to an invitation, and his diary was usually booked up for some time in advance. He seemed to have the talent of being, or appearing to be, in three places at once, and of doing at least two things at once, and doing them both very well. His future, like that of Bishop Marshall, must remain a matter for speculation, but it is unlikely that the authorities of the Church of England will allow him to remain as Bishop of Wakefield until his retirement.

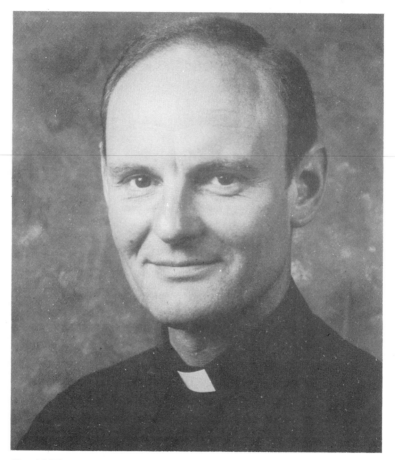

David Hutt, 12th Vicar, 1986–

CHAPTER TWELVE

THE AESTHETE
DAVID HUTT
1986–

*'The life of the Church has always provided a conscience for society.
. . . Just as our private and personal devotions, our rule of life and our practice as Christians are precious for the sake of the overall scheme, so the Church must act efficiently as a soul in a world made weary by hatred, greed and violence'*

(All Saints' Parish Paper, March 1988)

DAVID HANDLEY HUTT

Born: 24 August 1938

Royal Military Academy, Sandhurst 1958–60

The Queen's Royal Regiment 1960–1966

King's College, London 1966–1969

Deacon 1969   Priest 1970

Curate of St Michael and All Angels, Bedford Park
1969–1970

Curate of St Matthew's, Westminster 1970–1973

Priest Vicar and Succentor, Southwark Cathedral
1973–1978

Senior Chaplain, King's College, Taunton 1978–1982

Vicar of St Alban with St Patrick, Birminghan
1982–1986

Vicar of All Saints', Margaret Street 1986–

THE Reverend David Hutt, twelfth and present Vicar of All Saints, Margaret Street, has been in office for only two years at the time of writing, and any assessment of his ministry there will, of course, have to await a future biographer since this chapter is only just beginning. But for the sake of completeness, we have decided to include a brief account of his life. Fr Hutt himself has kindly provided us with much of the following material.

David Handley Hutt was born on 24 August 1938, the son of Frank and Evelyn Hutt. He was educated at Brentwood School, and from there pursued a career quite different from any of his eleven predecessors. He was accepted at the Royal Military Academy at Sandhurst for officer training, and was commissioned in the Queen's Royal Regiment, the 2nd Foot. The Regiment bears the Paschal Lamb as its cap badge, given to it by Queen Catherine, wife of Charles II, in 1661. He served with the Army from 1960 until 1966 when he decided that it was time to test a vocation to the priesthood. He trained at King's College, London, living initially in Cadogan Street, serving the daily Mass at St Mary's, Bourne Street, for Dr Eric Mascall, Professor of Historical Theology at King's. King's College at that time was staffed by people of the calibre of Mascall, Sydney Evans and Ulrich Simon.

The final year at King's College was spent living in the 'hothouse' atmosphere of the Theological Hostel in Vincent Square, Westminster, where he experienced some difficulty in coping with his fellow students, who were largely of a vociferous Anglo-Catholic tradition. This was followed by a thoroughly restful and enjoyable stay with the Community of the Servants of the Will of God at Crawley Down, a contemplative Cistercian community founded before the Second World War.

Ordination in 1969 was followed by a curacy at St

Michael and All Angels, Bedford Park, a Norman Shaw church set prominently in the garden suburb in west London designed by Shaw himself. The incumbent was a priest of the old school, entirely unsympathetic to the accommodation problems of his curate. The house had previously been occupied by a family who had sought to heat water by lighting newspapers under the bath, which had led to the partial collapse of the bathroom floor. This did not impress the incumbent who harangued his curate about his own experiences in the east end of London in the 1930s, having to climb up and down three flights of stairs to get water from a pump in the yard. No attempt had been made to assess the particular needs of Bedford Park and to formulate a strategy for visiting. Everything had to be done in the traditional way, whether or not it worked. St Michael and All Angels must have been one of the few remaining churches where the clergy said the Office of Sext together at 2 pm every afternoon. The year at Bedford Park was a time of profound unhappiness not helped by the seeming disinterest of the then Bishop of Kensington who had difficulty in remembering the names of the curates in his Episcopal area.

In 1970 David Hutt moved to be curate of St Matthew's, Westminster, under Gerard Irvine. The church was comparatively well attended and the interior was completely redecorated and reordered during his time there. The atmosphere of the church and parish was quite unlike that of a traditional parish church in a variety of ways and David Hutt likened it to 'living in a novel by Irish Murdoch'. At the invitation of the Dean of Westminster and the Headmaster of the Abbey Choir School, he taught the boys religious knowledge with some history and English.

St Matthew's was followed by five years as

Succentor of Southwark Cathedral, an administrative post concerned with the organization of the daily and special services in the Cathedral, and pastoral care of the Cathedral Choir. Two episodes were of special interest. A decision was taken to excavate the Cathedral crypt to make extra storage space. As the excavation was carried out, a pre-Saxon level was discovered including a Roman well of the 2nd century containing artefacts that had not been seen for nearly 2000 years. In 1976 the Cathedral was used as a film set for 'The Slipper and the Rose', a musical re-working of the story of Cinderella, starring Richard Chamberlain and Gemma Craven. David Hutt functioned as the Site Manager during the days of filming and found himself asked for help in dressing the bishop, played by the actor Geoffrey Bayldon.

In 1978, at the suggestion of the Vice-Provost of the Cathedral he replied to an advertisement in the *Church Times* for a Senior Chaplain at Taunton School. He spent four and a half happy years at the school which was the last of Canon Woodard's foundations. The school consisted of 550 boys, and attendance at Chapel on Sunday was compulsory. Holy Communion was not compulsory but it none-theless produced a remarkable attendance of 250. He taught for twenty-six periods a week with intellectually stimulating and committed professional colleagues whose life was teaching. One of his fellow schoolmasters was Timothy Whitworth, a grandson of William Allen Whitworth. An interest in education has been at the centre of his life since his days at Taunton.

Towards the end of his five-year contract at Taunton, he received an offer from Keble College, Oxford, asking him to consider the living of St Alban with St Patrick, Bordesley, in Birmingham. His abiding memories of his visit on a cold day were of mist, cobblestones and empty cans on the railings surrounding the church. St Alban's was a fine Pearson church with the addition of a 1930s tower and a good organ. It had been united with St Patrick's, a neighbouring church, also by Pearson but of no great merit, that had been demolished some years previously.

The parish presented certain problems to its new Vicar. The two previous incumbents, Dudley Clark and Lawrence Harding, had, between them, served the parish for fifty-nine years. The neighbourhood of slums – once the mission field of the brothers Pollock who had followed the example of the great slum priests of the early days of the Anglo-Catholic movement – had been demolished in the 1950s, leaving the church isolated from the remnants of its people as the slums and mean houses were replaced by that mixture of well spaced high and low rise blocks so typical of post war slum reclamation. The children at the Parish School were 60% Moslem, with a further 30% being Sikh, Hindu or Rastafarian. During his four-year incumbency, David Hutt secured the building of a parish hall and drew the church away from its rather idiosyncratic Anglo-Catholic tradition back into line with the Church of England.

The elevation of David Hope to the See of Wakefield meant that the right of presentation to the benefice of All Saints' reverted on this occasion to The Crown. Nevertheless the PCC and the Churchwardens were included informally in the consultation processes that led to the announcement from No. 10 Downing Street on 26 November 1985 that "The Queen has been pleased to approve that the Reverend David Hutt be appointed to the Vicarage of All Saints, St Marylebone". He left Birmingham with some sadness and was inducted as twelfth Vicar of All Saints', Margaret Street on Wednesday 14 May 1986.

Like all his predecessors David Hutt has already had to lead his congregation into a fresh onslaught on the financial problems that have faced the parish since its earliest days. Apart from the cost of maintaining the buildings so that the church may continue its witness and presence in the West End of London, funds need to be raised within the next decade to cover the cost of renewing the roof, a relatively unsuccessful experiment with aluminium in the post war years having proved to be a costly mistake. Further funds are needed for other essential repairs and for redecoration as the building is now showing its age, despite its massive construction and excellent workmanship.

While it would be premature to attempt any analysis of his ministry, already his innate sense of style and awareness of beauty have become apparent in the care he takes over the interior of the church, and his insistence on its rightful place as an integral part of the worship that is offered there day by day. His talents as a gardener in making the courtyard attractive and welcoming have been complemented by gifts as a flower arranger, neither usually associated with a Sandhurst graduate.

We will leave it to a future historian to assess his contribution to the ministry of this historic church of which he is the twelfth incumbent, but there are already developments pointing to the future. The moribund Institute of Christian Studies which enjoyed a brief existence in the years 1970–1978 had laid dormant in the years since, and its premises were let out to other uses. During his incumbency David Hope had given some thought to its future, but no firm decisions were made. His successor has encouraged the Trustees of the building (84 Margaret Street) to consider the possibility of reopening the Institute. Its future is still uncertain at the time of writing, and when reopened, is unlikely to resemble the former Institute because of increased competition from the many other Christian study centres which have developed in the years since it closed, but it is an interesting project and we wish it well. Since, in its latest regeneration, it will no longer have any formal connection with the church and parish which brought it into existence, further comment is outside the scope of this book.

Other moves include the development of the ministry of All Saints' to the commercial interests that now fill the parish boundaries to the exclusion of residents, as well as serving the needs of the gathered Sunday congregation. The midday masses are well attended and are followed by luncheon on some days of the week. A member of the weekday congregation has now been co-opted to the Parochial Church Council. A Christmas carol service for the employees of local businesses is a new and successful innovation. Members of this hitherto unknown and ignored part of the family of All Saints' are now attending the regular series of week night study courses.

It only remains for us to record the visit of the Most Reverend and Right Honourable Robert Alexander Runcie, 102nd Archbishop of Canterbury, to preach at the church on 1 November (All Saints Day) 1988. The words he has kindly written as the Foreword to this book, and his acceptance of the invitation to preach, indicate the value placed on this church and its ministry begun so modestly nearly 150 years ago by Frederick Oakeley on 5 July 1839.

EPILOGUE

In this book we have presented outlines of the life and ministry of each successive Vicar of All Saints' and attempted to discern those factors that characterised individual ministries, both those that were unique and those that they shared in some degree. But no parish priest can operate in a vacuum; the perceived success or failure of his ministry ultimately is determined by the total dialogue between him and those he serves and leads.

We have described some of the changes in the structure and geography of the parish and the congregation – the two are far from synonymous – these changes over the last 150 years have almost certainly made considerable demands on the Vicars and had equally major impact on the total contribution that All Saints' and its Vicars have been able to make to the mission of the Church of God.

Margaret Chapel and All Saints' itself were established in an impoverished area that demanded appropriate pastoral responses; that area has always been small. Only a few hundred yards square at its foundation, the parish was slightly expanded following the close of its neighbour, St. Andrew's Wells Street in 1931. The impetus for its foundation as a parish came from the eclectic congregation at Margaret Chapel who were sympathetic and responsive to the teaching of the founders of the Oxford Movement. Over the years there has been a depopulation of the area so that conventional parochial activities have become redundant, yet the Church has survived with relatively high numbers of worshippers in its regular congregation, apart from the countless visitors to the church or those who use it as their spiritual base when in London or England or those who come for counsel and advice.

The influence of the Oxford Movement has been such that almost every member of the regular Sunday congregation who comes to Margaret Street on a Sunday will have to pass several churches en route where there will be services of a similar churchmanship. It is that congregation that by and large provides the financial and personal support for the work of the church and as the lives of past Vicars have been unfolded we have seen how those congregations have been as faithful as their Vicars.

The appeal of All Saints' cannot be denied, neither can it be systematically analysed. The numinous character of the building itself, the particular tradition of worship, the high standard of music, the emphasis on teaching, the ministry of reconciliation, the regular round of the Daily Office and Eucharist, the *Opus Dei*; all these no doubt are important. Yet at the end we would have to conclude that it has been the sensitivity of the response by each successive Vicar to the contemporary needs of his flock and of the world that has successfully guided All Saints' since its foundation. If it be God's will, may it long continue. *Laus Deo*.

REFERENCES

PROLOGUE – FREDERICK OAKELEY

1 F. Oakeley, *Historical Notes on the Tractarian Movement* (London 1865), p. 59.
2 ibid., p. 62.
3 A. F. Bayford (ed.), *A Full Report of the Proceedings in the Case of the Office of the Judge Promoted by Hodgson v. Rev. F. Oakeley* (London, 1845), p. 167.
4 Court of Arches Records, H672/12.
5 A. F. Bayford, p. 167.

CHAPTER ONE – WILLIAM UPTON RICHARDS

1 *The Guardian,* 25 June 1873, p. 4.
2 Pusey Papers, Upton Richards to Pusey, Tuesday in the 2nd week of Advent 1845.
3 *The Church Times,* 30 June 1873.
4 *The Guardian,* 25 June 1873, pp. 2–3.
5 G. Body, *The Parting of Elijah and Elisha* (London, 1873).
6 F. Oakeley, *Popular Lectures, Personal Reminiscences of the 'Oxford Movement'* (London, 1855), pp. 11–12.

CHAPTER TWO – BERDMORE COMPTON

1 F. D. How, *Bishop Walsham How* (London, 1898), p. 89.
2 W. A. Whitworth, *Quam Dilecta* (London, 1891), p. 122.
3 *The Church Times,* 10 January 1908.
4 ibid.
5 ibid.
6 ibid.
7 *The Church Times,* 7 November 1873.
8 *Parish Paper,* February 1908.
9 W. A. Whitworth, *Quam Dilecta* (London, 1891), pp. 136–137.
10 ibid, p. 138.
11 Berdmore Compton, *The Fiftieth Year of the Reformantion of the Nineteenth Century* (London, 1883), p. 17.
12 ibid., pp. 32–33.
13 B. Compton, *Margin of Ceremonial and Moral Practice* (London 1874), pp. 10–11.
14 W. A. Whitworth, *Quam Dilecta* (London, 1891), p. 144.

15 *The Church Times,* 10 January 1908.

16 ibid.

17 ibid.

CHAPTER THREE – WILLIAM WHITWORTH

1 W. A. Whitworth, *Quam Dilecta* (London, 1891), p. 147.

2 *The Eagle,* Volume XXVI, 1905, p. 397.

3 ibid, p. 398.

4 W. A. Whitworth, *Quam Dilecta* (London, 1891).

5 *Parish Paper,* June 1898.

6 ibid, December 1886.

7 ibid, January 1887.

8 ibid, March 1887.

9 ibid, February 1888.

10 ibid, March 1888.

11 ibid, November 1888.

12 ibid.

13 ibid, February 1891.

14 ibid, October 1896.

CHAPTER FOUR – GEORGE HOLDEN

1 *The Church Times,* 13 March 1908.

2 Society of St Peter and St Paul, *St Peter's Eaton Square 1827–1927* (London, 1927), p. 15.

3 ibid, p. 16.

4 ibid.

5 ibid, p. 17.

6 *Parish Paper,* July 1905.

7 ibid.

8 ibid.

9 ibid.

10 ibid, March 1906.

11 ibid, June 1907.

CHAPTER FIVE – HENRY MACKAY

1 *The Church Times,* 24 April 1936.

2 *Parish Paper,* August 1908.

3 ibid.

4 ibid, December 1908.

5 Sidney Dark, *Mackay of All Saints'* (London, 1937), p. 93.

6   ibid, p. 126.
7   ibid, p. 105.
8   *The Church Times,* 24 April 1936.
9   Henry Mackay, *Assistants at the Passion* (London, 1929), p. 68.
10 ibid, p. 165.
11 Sidney Dark, *Mackay of All Saints'* (London, 1937), p. 148.
12 *The Church Times,* 1 May 1936.

CHAPTER SIX – BERNARD CLEMENTS

1   E. M. Almedingen, *Dom Bernard Clements* (London, 1945), p. 17.
2   ibid, p. 41.
3   ibid.
4   ibid, p. 52.
5   ibid, p. 53
6   ibid, p. 29.
7   G. E. F. Laing, *Dom Bernard Clements in Africa* (London, 1944), p. 52.
9   *Parish Paper,* August 1935.
10 ibid, February, 1936.
11 Dom Bernard Clements, *A Monk in Margaret Street* (London, 1941), pp. 123–124.
12 E. M. Almedingen, *Dom Bernard Clements* (London, 1945), p. 126.
13 ibid, p. 129.
14 Personal memories of Dr Hermia Mills.
15 *Parish Paper, December 1945.*
16 ibid.
17 E. M. Almedingen, *Dom Bernard Clements* (London, 1945), p. 91.

CHAPTER SEVEN – CYRIL TOMKINSON

1   H. Williams, *Some Day I'll Find You* (London, 1984), p. 114.
2   ibid, p. 115.
3   H. R. Williamson, *The Walled Garden* (London, 1956).
4   H. Williams, *Some Day I'll Find You* (London, 1984), p. 116.
5   *The Church Times,* 14 June 1968.

CHAPTER EIGHT – KENNETH ROSS

1   K. N. Ross, *Hearing Confessions* (London, 1974), Preface, p. vii.
2   ibid.
3   M. Hodgetts, 'Kenneth Needham Ross: The Margaret Street Years', *Christian* Volume 8 (1984), 33–40, p. 33.
4   K. N. Ross, *Why I Am Not a Roman Catholic* (London, 1953), p. 13.

5   *The Church Times,* 12 June 1970.

6   K. N. Ross, *Dangerous Delusions* (London, 1961), p. 65.

7   M. Hodgetts, 'Kenneth Needham Ross: The Margaret Street Years', *Christian,* Volume 8 (1984), p. 36.

8   ibid.

9   'ibid, p. 38.

10 ibid.

11 ibid, p. 39.

CHAPTER NINE – MICHAEL MARSHALL

1   M. Marshall, *Glory Under Your Feet* (London, 1978), p. 22.

2   ibid, p. 16

3   M. Marshall, *Renewal in Worship* (London, 1982), p. 10.

4   ibid.

5   ibid, p. 161.

6   Anglican Institute publicity leaflet, c. 1984.

CHAPTER TEN – DAVID SPARROW

1   *Parish Paper,* August 1981.

2   ibid, September 1981.

CHAPTER ELEVEN – DAVID HOPE

1   *Parish Paper,* December 1982.

2   ibid, January 1983.

3   ibid.

4   ibid, February 1983.

5   ibid, August 1983.

BIBLIOGRAPHY

ALL SAINTS' PARISH PAPER

ALMEDINGEN, E. M.
> *Dom Bernard Clements* (London, 1945).

BAYFORD, A. F. (ed.)
> *A Full Report of the Proceedings in the Case of the Office of the Judge Promoted by Hodgson v. Rev. F. Oakeley* (London, 1845).

BODY, G.
> *The Parting of Elijah and Elisha* (London, 1873).

THE CHURCH TIMES

CLEMENTS, Dom Bernard
> *Christ and Everyman,* ed. E. Sillitoe (London, 1946).
>
> *A Monk in Margaret Street* (London, 1941).

COMPTON, Berdmore
> *The Fiftieth Year of the Reformation of the Nineteenth Century* (London, 1883).
>
> *Margin of Ceremonial and Moral Practice* (London, 1874).

DARK, Sidney
> *Mackay of All Saints'* (London, 1937).

THE EAGLE

THE GUARDIAN

HOLDEN, George F.
> *The Holy Ghost the Comforter* (London, 1908).
>
> *The Special Bases of the Anglican Claim* (London, 1903).

HOPE, David M.
> *The Leonine Sacramentary* (Oxford, 1970).

HOW, F. D.
> *Bishop Walsham How* (London, 1898).

LAING, G. E. F.
Dom Bernard Clements in Africa (London, 1944).
MACKAY, Henry F. B.
Assistants at The Passion (London, 1929).
The Message of Francis of Assisi (London, 1924).
The Religion of the Englishman (London, 1911).
Saints and Leaders (London, 1928).
The Twelve Gates (London, 1933).
MARSHALL, Michael E.
Glory Under Your Feet (London, 1978).
Renewal in Worship (London, 1982).
OAKELEY, Frederick
Historical Notes on the Tractarian Movement (London, 1865).
Popular Lectures, Personal Reminiscences of the 'Oxford Movement' (London, 1865).
ROSS, Kenneth N.
Dangerous Delusions (London, 1961).
Hearing Confessions (London, 1974).
Letter to a Homosexual (London, 1955).
Why I Am Not a Roman Catholic (London, 1953).
SOCIETY OF ST PETER AND ST PAUL
St Peter's Eaton Square 1827–1927 (London, 1927).
THE TIMES
WHITWORTH, William A.
Quam Dilecta (London, 1891).
WILLIAMS, Harry
Some Day I'll Find You (London, 1984).
WILLIAMSON, H. Ross
The Walled Garden (London, 1956).

INDEX

239

241